D1179146

This book
belongs to:

Patrick Graat

Happy Christmas

from

Margaret 25. 12. 05

HOLLYWOOD
A CELEBRATION!

HOLLYWOOD
A CELEBRATION!

DAVID THOMSON

Photographs from The Kobal Collection

London, New York, Munich,
Melbourne, Delhi

Project Editor and Photo Research/Editor: Barbara M. Berger
Designer: Timothy Shaner, Night & Day Design

Senior Art Editor: Michelle Baxter
Creative Director: Tina Vaughan
Jacket Director: Dirk Kaufman
Publisher: Sean Moore
Editorial Director: Chuck Wills
Production Manager: Chris Avgherinos
DTP Designer: Russell Shaw
Editorial Assistant: Crystal Coble

Published in the United States by
DK Publishing, Inc.
375 Hudson Street
New York, New York 10014

A Penguin Company

First American Edition, 2001
00 01 02 03 04 05 10 9 8 7 6 5 4 3 2 1

Dorling Kindersley Publishing, Inc. offers special discounts for bulk purchases for sales
promotions or premiums. Specific, large-quantity needs can be met with special editions,
including personalized covers, excerpts of existing guides, and corporate imprints.
For more information, contact Special Markets Department, Dorling Kindersley Publishing, Inc.,
95 Madison Avenue, New York, NY 10016 Fax: 800-600-9098.

Library of Congress Cataloging-in-Publication Data

Thomson, David, 1941-
    Hollywood : a celebration / David Thomson.
      p. cm.
    Includes index.
    ISBN 0-7894-7792-0 (alk. paper)
      1. Motion pictures--United States--Pictorial works. 2. Motion
picture actors and actresses--United States--Portraits.   I. Title.
    PN1993.5.U65 T55 2001
    791.43'75'0973--dc21

                                        2001032452

Reproduced by Colourscan Ltd., Singapore
Printed and bound in Singapore by Star Standard Industries (Pte.) Ltd

See our complete catalog at
www.dk.com

Contents

1939. There's no place like home. In *The Wizard of Oz*, Dorothy's ruby slippers *(right)* were magical—and with only four pairs from the movie known to exist, they are quite valuable as well—a pair was auctioned in May 2000 for $666,000.

1926. Early Hollywood stars pose *(previous pages)* during a summer party held at actress Constance Talmadge's Malibu beach house. The photo ran in the October 1926 issue of *Motion Picture Magazine*. *From left to right, on fence:* Roscoe "Fatty" Arbuckle, Mae Murray, Ward Crane, Virginia Valli, Ronald Colman, Bessie Love, Jack Pickford, Rudolph Valentino, and Pola Negri. *Scattered through the middle row:* Louella O. Parsons, Carmel Myers, Alan Forrest, Bert Lytell, Claire Windsor, Dick Barthelmess, Constance Talmadge (hatless, in center), Beatrice Lillie, Josephine Lovett, Julanne Johnstone, Agnes Ayres, John S. Robertson, and Marshall Neilan. *Bottom row includes:* Antonio Moreno, Prince David Divani, Charles Lane, Alf Goulding, Marcel De Sano, Manuel Reachi (Agnes Ayres's husband), Harry d'Abbadie d'Arrast, Natalie Talmadge Keaton, Captain Alastair MacIntosh (Constance Talmadge's husband), Mrs. Antonio Moreno, and Blanche Sweet.

Introduction

by David Thomson

New Ideas in a New Land

To begin before the beginning. There have been great moments in the modern or recent history of mankind when southern California was little more than desert There were cultures, kingdoms, and civilizations in China, Babylon and Egypt; there was the Italian Renaissance; there was the Age of Enlightenment; there was Napoleon Bonaparte—and still the Western colonization of southern California, let alone the founding of Hollywood, had hardly yet begun. After all, until 1848 the entire region was part of Mexico—the most remote—with a few dozen missions, several forts, a little citrus farming, and the native Americans.

c. 1920. The former William Fox Studios in Hollywood (*above*), on Sunset Boulevard and Western Avenue.

1939. Crowds arrive at the Loew's Grand in Atlanta on December 15 for the premiere of *Gone with the Wind (left).*

We are talking of just over 150 years ago, when it is estimated that the population in the area that is now greater Los Angeles was about 2,500. By 1895—which happens to be the year in which the thing we call movies or cinema or film was first shown to an audience (in Paris)—the population was still only 150,000.

In 1895, the world (or a very small section of it) saw Oscar Wilde's *The Importance of Being Earnest* for the first time: it was a hot new play, not a classic. The same year, the Sino-Japanese War ended, and in its defeat China was obliged to give "Formosa" to Japan. Formosa is now called Taiwan, and it could cause hostility between a very different China and a much-altered United States. In 1895, Joseph Conrad published *Almayer's Folly*; Thomas Hardy wrote *Jude the Obscure*; Mark Twain's *Pudd'nhead Wilson* was a fashionable success. There was no such thing as air travel, television, or computers—and there was nowhere called Hollywood.

Introduction

1895. This shot of a live steam engine revolutionized the moving picture: from *L'Arrivée d'un train à la Ciotat,* by Auguste and Louis Lumière.

This is not a game. It is a way of saying that in the spectrum of time it was just yesterday, really (as measured against the "reality" handed down to us by such a movie marvel as *Jurassic Park*), that the experience of people "just like us" was so very different. And when it comes to measuring or describing that difference, it is not enough to say that movies were, simply, a new form of entertainment, or the first mass medium. They were those things, and that is vital to our understanding of them. But the movies were something more profound (and far harder to assess): They were a way of altering our relationship to reality. And in the long term, who knows if that is not what they will be remembered for?

In that Paris screening in 1895, a fascinating thing occurred. The inventors, Auguste and Louis Lumière (the sons of a still photographer from Lyons), had a few fragments of film shot in order to prove that their camera/projector, the "cinematographe," worked. They had not "written" or "directed" their fragments. They attempted no story. They had merely searched for some subject that showed movement and duration.

So they shot workers leaving a factory, a family having a picnic, and a train coming into a depot.

In that last fragment, a modest steam engine chugged slowly in the direction of the camera. Some in the audience screamed, got up, and ran from the dark, believing that the engine would come out of the screen and strike them down.

Comic? Absurd? Primitive? I told you, experience was different then. These people were like us, but not the same as us. And yet, in 1975, when the white arm reached out of the cindery grave in *Carrie*, people jumped. Maybe you were there. I stood at the back of a theater and observed that audiences, literally, rose, a foot or more, in and from their seats. Is it ridiculous to think there is life up there on the screen? When you saw *Erin Brockovich* did you fall in love with Julia Roberts? Or, after *Titanic*, did you take Leonardo DiCaprio home in your head, and keep him alive in your dreams?

Insane? Well, don't rule that possibility out just because "everyone" is subject to the screen's compelling fantasies. I did say that our sense of reality was involved.

1993. Tom Hanks won an Oscar for his role as lawyer Andrew Beckett, seen here in a still from *Philadelphia,* directed by Jonathan Demme.

And so, try to imagine the report of scientists from centuries far in the future—more than centuries, millennia—who come upon our debris and say: "These dots were in the habit of inhaling intense reproductions of reality—very touching, very funny, very violent, very sexy—and fantasizing over them. It is remarkable that they seem not to have noticed any change in their actual dealings with reality, no matter that their world became increasingly emotional, comic, violent, and sexual. Alas, the dots succumbed to the instability that resulted."

Now, I know, that sounds foreboding—but just because this book is a "celebration" is no reason to exclude all worrying questions, or those gotchas like locomotives that might land in your lap. The movies are too potent and far-reaching for us to act like idiots delighted at being entertained. After all, movies show us so many more things than the beautiful faces of stars to fall in love with. It was moving film, or video, every night on television that gave the American public a conscience, and doubts, about the war in Vietnam. If film had been so developed in 1914, and

if there had been television then, would the slaughter of trench warfare in Flanders have lasted four years? Every time famine or disaster in remote countries is shown to us, our giving mounts; yet every time some famous outrage is rerun, the more jaded we become. Voyeurism may increase sentimental response, but perhaps it diminishes responsibility.

Consider that paradox, and film becomes so much more than entertainment. There is always a documentary function at work (whether or not that label is employed). *Traffic* may make us understand the drug trade better, just as *Philadelphia* made us more aware of AIDS and the specious fears it prompted.

It is often hard to tell whether movies lead or follow society, but Hollywood's growing ease with black life is a significant part of the nation's improved race relations. It is also one reason why the Civil War epic *The Birth of a Nation* (1915)—a film of the highest historical importance—can hardly be shown today without extensive warning that D. W. Griffith, its director and visionary, was a racist. *Gone with the Wind,* nowadays, makes many people wince. Yet it still works

1916. D. W. Griffith (in hat) on set during the filming of *Intolerance;* after *The Birth of a Nation,* the director explored the theme of inhumanity throughout the ages.

Introduction

as entertainment. Like any study of history, a close look at the movies only reminds us how much our perspective can change.

Hollywood (in the sense of a particular area of Los Angeles) came into being where this book begins, around 1915, the year *Birth of a Nation* opened and signaled the beginning of a great medium. Before then, movies were 10 or 20 minutes long. Griffith's film was over three hours, with developed stories. Vast audiences of all classes came to see it—as if they were going to the theater. It is still, in all likelihood, the most successful film ever made in terms of profit. One man who shared in its success was Louis B. Mayer, a Russian immigrant who owned a few movie theaters in New England. He bought the local distribution rights to *Birth of a Nation* and did so well that in less than ten years he was a part of Metro-Goldwyn-Mayer, the greatest of all the movie studios. In those days before sound, most of America went to the movies regularly. Of course, the population then was lower (along with the ticket prices), but the habit of moviegoing was still a fresh thrill, so one should remember the intense adoration given to stars like Chaplin and Garbo, and the way in which their image was known all over the world. That kind of celebrity had previously been allowed only to kings and religious leaders—and never with the amazing illusion of intimacy that comes from beholding Garbo's face filling a wall twenty feet high.

Some argued that the movies hurt themselves and their sway by adding sound—there was a purity and beauty to the silent imagery, and also a powerful unity in a nation where many people's English was uncertain. Today, we have been through so many other changes—adding color, boosting the screen size, absorbing television, video, the VCR, the DVD, and computer-generated imagery—that we must see how far change is a constant. But that only prompts one to think where the medium is headed. Moviegoing, as such, is no longer the habit it once was. But the impact of moving imagery is continual and ubiquitous. It is

1928. With the advent of sound, audiences could hear MGM's famous trademark lion, Leo, roar for the first time. In this photograph, Leo poses for his close-up.

1990s. The fifty-foot-tall landmark Hollywood sign was erected in Beachwood Canyon in 1923. Originally a real estate ad, until 1945 it read "Hollywoodland."

not really too fanciful to suppose that camera language could supplant that of words. Just consider how much more time your children spend looking at pictures than reading.

I make these points so that the entertainment value of the movies may be placed in context. Yet this is now a world in which anyone saying "Casablanca" likely means the movie, not the place. And "Hollywood"—all over the world—is not the small neighborhood, but the kingdom of the movies and a synonym for Americana. As such, the movie has been as much a measure of empire as the roads, the law, and the army were for Rome. It is the movies that make many foreigners think that America is foolish, immature, and sensationalistic, and it is the movies that have helped make people from all over the world so eager to get to America.

It is simpleminded to say that the movies have been simple entertainment. Indeed, their effortless opening up of dreamscape and inner desires is complex and ambiguous. We are all used to being wary of violence on the screen. Does it help release dangerous urges, or does it give unhappy kids something to imitate? We should examine all the evidence on such matters just because the questions are hard to answer. But what is asked far less often is what has been the influence of so many movies about romance—teaching us how to kiss, urging us to fall in love, and laying in such an unattainable code for happiness? Has that stress made for more love? Or more divorce? Entertainment works at so many levels.

It depends on who you are. If you're the director (anyone from Frank Capra to Francis Ford Coppola) then film may be a work of art. If you're the studios, film is a product on which you require a profit. You are in a business, and you may battle with the director if he wants a three-hour film instead of a two-hour one (because that means one less screening a day). But if you're you, the audience, then you reckon you've bought the film (for 10¢ or $10), and you want to be transported—you want the kind of involvement you've had with, say, *King Kong*, *The Wizard of Oz*, *It's a Wonderful Life*, *Singin' in the Rain*, *Some Like It Hot*,

Introduction

1930s. An early movie audience is transfixed by the gigantic visage of Ginger Rogers, during a screening of one of her many films.

The Sound of Music, *Bonnie and Clyde*, *The Godfather*, *Jaws*, *Star Wars*, *E.T.*, and so on. Those are classics, so popular that any claim of art hardly matters, yet so appealing to so many people that their profit is irrelevant as well.

Historically, as movies began, people like Chaplin (essentially uneducated) were excited by the thought of a storytelling medium for everyone—not just those who read Conrad and Hardy (a tiny minority). That philosophy means art for everyone, not just an educated elite. Elites resent that, and ambitious filmmakers and lofty critics are alike in that they like to think of films rivaling novels and poetry.

But is there any real need for that? Do the movies need to be an art if so many people enjoy them?

That said, Hollywood, since 1915, has produced well over 20,000 movies. Not even the wildest celebration could like them all. Many are lost, and likely deserve to be. (Equally, the list of those lost includes pictures that people once regarded as classics.) This book picks out

a little over 900—a small fraction. There could be more. Most of your favorites will be here, but not all. Choices were made, which means that many were passed over, whereas another compiler would have included them. In other words, it's not going too far to say that, since 1915, several thousand movies have been made that you could watch tonight with pleasure. They're not all great; they may not match *King Lear*, Rembrandt's self-portraits, or Mozart's operas. But they still work and delight. That is an extraordinary achievement, and it begins to suggest how far the movie has enlarged all our imaginations.

So turn over the following pages. Bring back the memories. Remember titles you may never have heard of. Keep a list for trips to the local video store—for many of these 900 are available somewhere. And they are waiting for you.

1910s. Master storyteller Charlie Chaplin ended many films with this iconic shot of himself as the "Little Tramp" ambling alone down an empty country road.

1915-29

1910s–1920s. Outstandingly popular in the early days of Hollywood were the films of the Keystone Kops *(right)*, featuring elaborate and spectacular car chases made all the easier by the long and still empty streets of Los Angeles.

1915–29

Golden Age of Silents

1929. If this book had been compiled in 1927, this beauty might not have gained admission. For then, Louise Brooks *(left, in The Canary Murder Case)* was one starlet among many. But her career was changed when the German director, G. W. Pabst, asked her to go to Berlin to make *Pandoras's Box* (1929). Today, we look at that film and see that the very frank face from Cherryvale, Kansas, was an icon of the 1920s.

1923. There were many great comedians in the silent era, and one of the greatest was Harold Lloyd *(previous pages)*. Working for the Hal Roach Studios, Lloyd played a decent, ordinary guy who specialized in hair-raising stunts and scrapes. He is seen here in one of his most suspenseful films, *Safety Last*, where he also climbs a twelve-story building without the benefit of camera tricks or stuntmen.

Young people today may think that the age of silent cinema was too long ago to concern them. Let the vitality and drama of the images on the next few pages challenge that attitude. Amazingly, it was in the 1920s that the largest proportion of Americans went to the movies. Hollywood had only lately asserted itself as the central location from which movies might come. And as America took its place in international affairs by entering the First World War, it is hard to underestimate the significance of the director D. W. Griffith. With *The Birth of a Nation* and *Intolerance* he made the motion picture something everyone needed to see. President Woodrow Wilson saw *Birth of a Nation* and called it "history written in lightning."

It would be an era of superb clowns, producing three comic masters—Charlie Chaplin, Buster Keaton, and Harold Lloyd—who still amaze. If the whole world laughed at Charlie, wasn't there hope for unity and compassion? There were fabulous stars—like Rudolph Valentino, Douglas Fairbanks, Mary Pickford, and Gloria Swanson. There were great directors and showmen—Mack Sennett, Cecil B. DeMille, Erich von Stroheim—and so many movies that have not survived, because the companies that made them were careless, or because the pictures were not always very good. But there were monumental achievements, too, not just films for the movie buff but pictures that still move modern audiences—*Greed, Ben-Hur, Sunrise,* and *The Crowd.*

Above all, this was the original age of going into the dark, when the swirl of action and the hopefulness of young faces blazed on screen, and when the world began to realize the passion of its wakeful dreaming.

1915–29

1910s. In 1914, when films were one- or two-reelers (no longer than thirty minutes), the Mack Sennett Studios were a center of the Los Angeles movie world. This is where Charlie Chaplin would work. Note that some of the studio space is roofless to allow the natural light inside.

1910s. Mack Sennett was born as Michael Sinnott in Canada in 1880, the child of Irish immigrants. As the founder and head of the Keystone studio, he worked with nearly every great silent clown—writing, directing, and producing hundreds of films. Sennett was still active in the 1930s producing W. C. Fields's pictures. In 1937 he was given one of the first honorary Oscars for being "the master of fun, discoverer of stars." He died in California at the age of 80.

1910s–1920s. Californian beaches were an inspiration—then and now—for new swimwear, and the lack of it. Mack Sennett liked to keep a gang of pretty young women at the studio to enliven both on- and off-set productions. He called them the Bathing Beauties *(left)*, and they established that essential duty of the movies (long before thinness was in): to show a little bit of young flesh.

1910s–1920s. Sennett said the girls were beautiful but dumb *(above)*. But plenty of them were smart enough to promote their careers: actresses like Marie Prevost, Phyllis Haver, and even Carole Lombard had begun that way. Some said Gloria Swanson had been a Bathing Beauty. "Oh no!" she declared. "Why, I couldn't even swim!"

1910s. Roscoe "Fatty" Arbuckle *(right)* was already a highly paid star by the time Chaplin arrived. A popular figure in screen slapstick, his career was shattered in 1921 after he was accused of raping an actress-cum-call girl who became ill during his party at a San Francisco hotel on Labor Day and died four days later. Arbuckle was acquitted after three trials, but he never quite recovered from the scandal, and died in 1933 at the age of 46.

1910s. Charles Chaplin (born in South London in 1889, and raised in conditions of Dickensian poverty) was on his way to becoming the best-known man in the world. Soon after his arrival in Los Angeles, he met the Sennett star Mabel Normand *(right)*, who would be Chaplin's partner in many of his early short films.

1910s. Some comics were just clowns who did their routines in front of the camera. But Chaplin was the complete, obsessive filmmaker *(left)*. He decided where the camera should be, and he was tireless enough at the end of the day to sit down and begin his own editing. He was also startlingly beautiful.

1916. This is Chaplin at the Mutual Studio in Hollywood in *One A.M (right)*, a short that was derived from one of his greatest music-hall acts—a drunk who returns home in the early hours and has to negotiate the house without waking anyone.

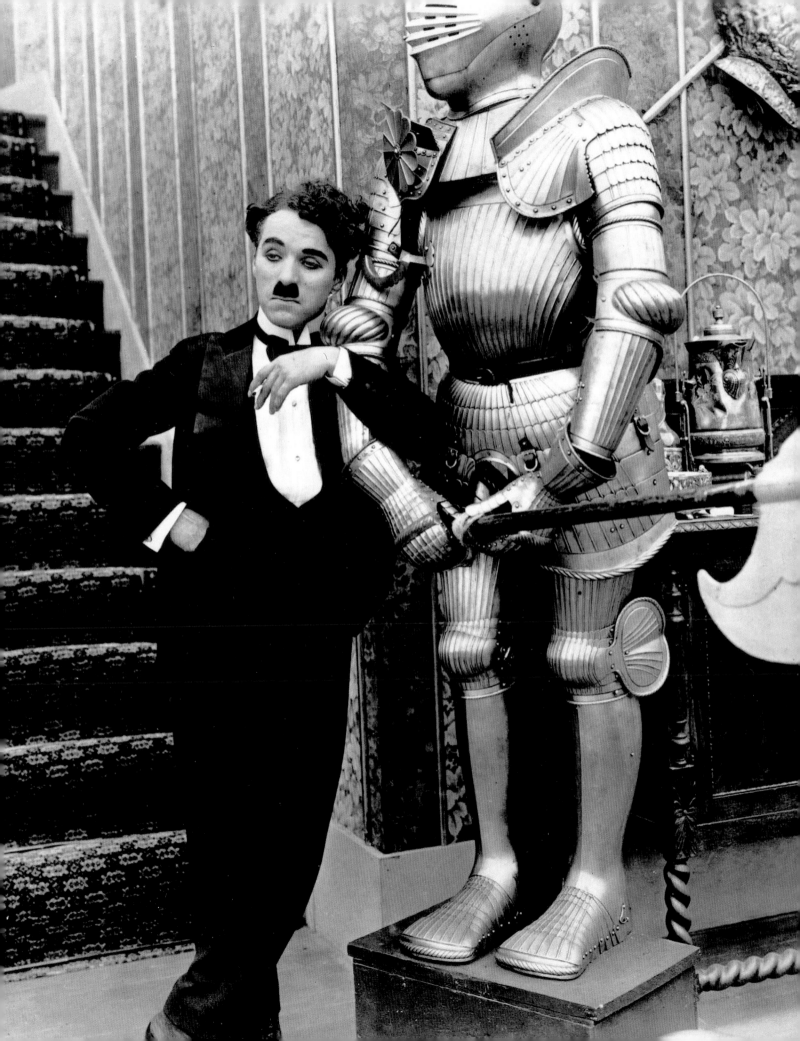

1910s. Here is Chaplin again, clowning around on set for a publicity shot. But, in truth, he loved cameras and what they could do. And from 1923 onward (with *A Woman in Paris*), Chaplin shot his films with his own money, so that he could keep shooting and reshooting until he was sure he had everything right.

1919. Chaplin made the three-reeler *Shoulder Arms* for First National Pictures, and turned the recent horrors of war into slapstick. In six years, he had gone from earning $150 a week to a contract of over a million dollars for eight short films.

1925. Chaplin opened *The Gold Rush* in 1925, after extensive location work in the Sierra Nevada mountains. At last, he was working for the United Artists company he had helped found—and *The Gold Rush* grossed over $6 million.

1916. David Wark Griffith had known actors most of his life. He had tried the job himself. So as a director, he acted the part: he was tall, but he wore a hat; he might be worried, but he seemed unconcerned and gradually the message spread—that Mr Griffith was in charge. Griffith *(left)* is on the set of *Intolerance*.

1915. Born in La Grange, Kentucky, in 1875, Griffith was the son of a Confederate cavalry colonel. He had tried the theater, but never flourished. But from 1908 onward, he made, literally, hundreds of short movie melodramas in which he gradually refined the narrative power of the medium. Here he is during the filming of *Birth of a Nation (above),* taking a lunch break, reading the paper, and chatting with one of his actors, Robert Harron.

1915. **A master** of the close-up, Griffith also had a fond eye for long shots where the eye is led by the action and the natural varieties of light, as in this battle scene from *Birth of a Nation (left)*. Just as *Gone with the Wind* would be, it is a story of how the Civil War affected the South.

1915. **Henry Walthall** leads a Civil War attack in *Birth of a Nation (right)*, in a dramatic still that could be a shot from a modern film or newsmagazine, with the thrust directed at the camera. Griffith was one of those directors who invented the use of the telling detail as a vehicle for emotional impact.

1915. **George Seigmann** pursues Mae Marsh in *Birth of a Nation (left)*, in a scene typical of Griffith's films and many other silents, where virtuous young women were put to grievous tests, over and over again. Some people wondered: did cinema really mean to protect virgins? Or was it taking advantage of the threat to them?

1915. Griffith took enormous pains over historical research and the remaking of sets that were true to the original sites. Griffith is the white-coated figure surveying the construction of the Ford's Theatre set for *Birth of a Nation*.

1915. Here is the finished stage set in action, during the scene just before the assassination of President Lincoln. Lincoln was played by Joseph Henabery and John Wilkes Booth by Raoul Walsh, who would have a long career as a director.

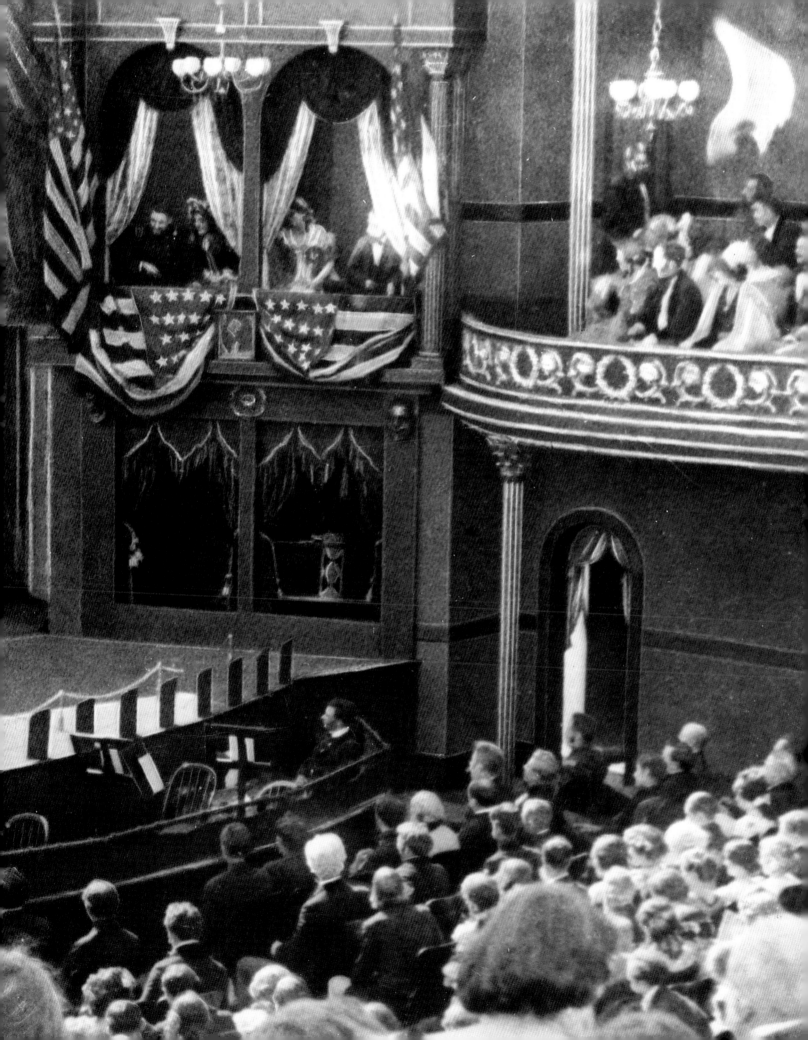

1916. Lillian Gish was Griffith's favorite actress, and one of the great faces of silent cinema. She had been in *Birth of a Nation*, and she would play lead parts in *True Heart Susie, Way Down East, Broken Blossom,* and *Orphans of the Storm.* But in *Intolerance (left)* she was, quite simply, the "Woman Who Rocks the Cradle of Time," a recurring image in the face of all manner of cruelty.

1916. The set of Babylon built by Griffith for *Intolerance (previous pages)* was massive. At that time it loomed over most of the rest of Los Angeles, and there were those who wanted it preserved as a civic monument. But in Los Angeles, new sets replace old with startling speed. In addition, *Intolerance* did far less well at the box office than expected.

1918. Griffith liked to work with a close-knit team that often included the same actors and crew from project to project. In this off-set photograph *(above)*, he is shooting *Hearts of the World* with actress Josephine Crowell and his trusted cameraman, Billy Bitzer. A huge column from the *Intolerance* set can be seen in the upper left-hand corner, and there, off to the right, is assistant Erich von Stroheim, making sure the military uniforms are correct.

1910s. Lillian Gish was the ideal, virtuous woman in Griffith's view of melodrama *(above),* and she was a great star for a few years. But by the mid-1920s she was thought to be too prim, and she gradually became a character actress.

1917. The Gish character was challenged from as early as 1917 by this Cincinnati girl, Theodosia Goodman *(right, in Cleopatra),* whose stage name was Theda Bara (arrange the letters, said her publicists, and the name became "Arab death").

1917. Cleopatra had one of her first movie adventures as a Theda Bara vehicle *(right).* The film was produced by William Fox (born Wilhelm Fried in Hungary), who went from the garment business to the movie industry. He is the "Fox" in 20th Century Fox films and the Fox Television network.

WILLIAM FOX PRESENTS

Theda Bara

-IN-

CLEOPATRA

STAGED BY
J. GORDON EDWARDS

FOX FILM
CORPORATION

A THEDA BARA
SUPER
PRODUCTION

1924. In the early days of movies, the poster was discovered for press advertising and lobby display. It was not always photographic then (this poster for *The Thief of Baghdad, left,* is a painted illustration), but it was a way into the business for kids who had a visual imagination. And gradually, the art of storyboarding became important—a series of drawings that worked like a script.

1924. Douglas Fairbanks in one of his most successful roles *(above)*, as *The Thief of Baghdad,* in a costume designed by Mitchell Leisen (a good director of the 1930s and 1940s). He was the epitome of energy and daring. Only 56 when he died, Fairbanks is still considered the reigning master at conveying the exhilaration of movement.

1924. Anna May Wong keeps an eye on Fairbanks (who was always the roguish gentleman) in *The Thief of Bagdad (right)*. Born in the Los Angeles Chinatown, her role as the slave girl opposite Fairbanks made her a star.

1920s. Douglas Fairbanks, always ready to have his picture taken, in the backyard of one of the homes he and Mary Pickford shared (*above*). Fairbanks was never content with ordinary movement—he leaped, he bounded, and he did most of his own stunts.

1920s. A very real couple, and for a few years close to perfect (*left*): America's sweetheart (born in Canada), Mary Pickford, and the great swashbuckling hero of the silent screen, "Doug" Fairbanks. They did amazing work selling war bonds, and that image carried over—for several years, at least—in the first great celebrity marriage.

1917. Second only to Chaplin in popularity, and at least his equal in matters of business, this is Pickford playing the young teenage lead in *Rebecca of Sunnybrook Farm (right)*, although she was 24 years old at the time. The grown Pickford resented having to play children, but public adoration kept her acting in young roles into her 30s.

1925. Always arrogant and willful, Erich von Stroheim rose swiftly, and in 1923–24 he filmed the novel *McTeague* by Frank Norris. The movie was called *Greed*, and it is a masterpiece of psychological realism, with a desperate finale in Death Valley *(above)*.

1925. When *Greed* was finished it ran 8 hours. The production head at Metro-Goldwyn-Mayer, Irving Thalberg, had it cut down to 2 hours. *Greed* is excessive, disturbing, full of genius—and a monument to hubris. Here are Zasu Pitts and Gibson Gowland *(left)* as the married couple ruined by dreams of wealth.

1922. One of the first great pretenders in the film business: he is either Erich von Stroheim, Prussian, aristocratic, and an officer under the Kaiser; or Erich Stroheim, Jewish, a hatter's son from Vienna. In this still *(right)*, von Stroheim plays the cruel aristocrat in *Foolish Wives—* "the man you love to hate".

1928. Von Stroheim directing Fay Wray in *The Wedding March* *(above)*. Most of his later films ran into trouble, partly because of the Von's urge to introduce perverse sexuality into his films. For all that, people like Fay Wray said he was a marvel, and a very funny man quite clear on how he was ruining his own great career.

1920s. Von Stroheim remained a director, an actor, a self-destructive force, and perhaps the most fascinating figure in silent cinema *(left)*. But you know that great face already—if you remember *Sunset Boulevard* (1950).

1928. *Queen Kelly* was Stroheim's swansong *(right)*. He was hired to direct by coproducers Gloria Swanson (getting whipped here by Seena Owen) and her lover, Joseph Kennedy. In the end they had to fire him, but the restored version of *Queen Kelly* is like *Greed*—a great film that might have been greater.

1920s. Another giant of the silent screen: Lon Chaney *(left),* a boy who grew up in Colorado telling stories to his deaf-mute mother, and went on to become a great mime and a master of make-up—the "Man of a Thousand Faces."

1925. One of Chaney's great hits was *The Phantom of the Opera (below),* in which he costarred with Mary Philbin. While having every wish to scare us, Chaney was one of the first actors to identify with hideous monsters and scarred souls.

1923. So many of the great roles of horror and melodrama were done by Chaney first, including Quasimodo in *The Hunchback of Notre Dame (right).* Chaney died of cancer in 1930, when he was only 47.

1921. His real name was Rodolfo Alfonzo Raffaele Pierre Filiberto Guglielmi di Valentina D'Antonguolla, but the business reckoned that "Rudolph Valentino" played better. It was a short, sensational career in which he was famous as the great lover, but a good deal more gender-confused in private. In *The Sheik (above)*, with Agnes Ayres in the female lead, he flirted with notions of rape, sex, and Arab identity.

1926. If you have a hit, make a sequel: in the very earliest days of film the business had no shame in repeating itself *(right)*. Struck down in 1926, Valentino had time for only 14 major films. But his name survives in folklore.

1921. Valentino was really launched—doing the tango— in *Four Horsemen of the Apocalypse (left)*, directed by the brilliant Rex Ingram and scripted by June Mathis—one of the behind-the-scenes women vital to Valentino's career.

John W. Considine, Jr. presents

RUDOLPH VALENTINO
in "The Son of the Sheik"
a Sequel to 'The Sheik'

with VILMA BANKY

from the novel by E. M. HULL — Adapted to the Screen by FRANCES MARION

A GEORGE FITZMAURICE PRODUCTION
- UNITED ARTISTS PICTURE -

1924. Ernst Lubitsch was one of the great directors of German cinema. In 1921, he came to America (to direct Mary Pickford and make her grown-up). That didn't work, but Lubitsch stayed and redefined comedy. Here is a scene from *Forbidden Paradise (left)*, with Pola Negri and Rod La Rocque.

1919. *Cecil B. DeMille* loved women and clothes. In his version of the 1918 film *The Admirable Crichton*—entitled *Male and Female*—he had Gloria Swanson, seen here with Thomas Meighan *(right)*, washed ashore on a desert island (in a drenched, clinging dress) and then dreaming of herself in exotic clothes. This is a hallowed Hollywood tradition—having your cake and eating it too.

1925. DeMille guessed that his audiences shared his fascination with marriage, infidelity, and temptation. Scenes such as this one from the "candy ball" in *The Golden Bed*—with Lillian Rich as the marshmallow-covered lamp to male attention—were thrillingly decadent fantasies. Interestingly, *The Golden Bed* was the first film with costumes designed by the legendary Hollywood designer Edith Head.

1920s. From the early 1920s to the late 1950s, people knew the names of very few movie directors. But they knew Cecil B. DeMille—because he was the best self-promoter. Hence this publicity still of "CB" (in riding breeches) explaining the world to four great stars: Bebe Daniels, Agnes Ayres, Gloria Swanson, and Wanda Hawley.

1927. Sooner or later, DeMille was bound to take on the Bible. This is *The King of Kings*, with H. B. Walthall as Christ and Joseph Schildkraut (on the far right) as Judas Iscariot.

1927. The selling point to all Biblical stories is the adjacency of a great deal of sin and depravity alongside the secure message of salvation: Here is Jacqueline Logan as Mary Magdalene, with thoughts of sin in *The King of Kings*.

1923. DeMille also loved décor and art direction—showing us places from our dreams. This is Charles De Roche as the Pharaoh in *The Ten Commandments*—the role played by Yul Brynner when DeMille remade the subject in 1956.

1923. On the subject of sin, here is Estelle Taylor (who would later marry heavyweight champ Jack Dempsey) getting hot and bothered with the golden calf in *The Ten Commandments*.

1920s. By the mid-1920s, Metro-Goldwyn-Mayer was a power in Hollywood, and here are four of its power-brokers, from left to right: Louis B. Mayer, head of the West Coast operation; Marion Davies, movie star and mistress to William Randolph Hearst, and an MGM property; Norma Shearer, another major star at the studio; and Irving G. Thalberg, her husband, and chief of production.

1928. Marion Davies was a fine comic actress, and *Show People*, directed by King Vidor, was one of her biggest hits. It tells the story of a country girl who comes to Hollywood and has a surprise success.

1926. Louis B. Mayer took his family to Europe in the early 1920s. One of the things he discovered there was a Swedish actress, Greta Gustafsson. In America she would be Garbo, and here she is on the set of *Flesh and the Devil* with her costar, the American matinee idol John Gilbert (far right), and Swedish actor Lars Hanson, also found on the trip.

1926. Garbo and Gilbert set the screen on fire together in Clarence Brown's *Flesh and the Devil*. But there was a far more torrid love affair in private.

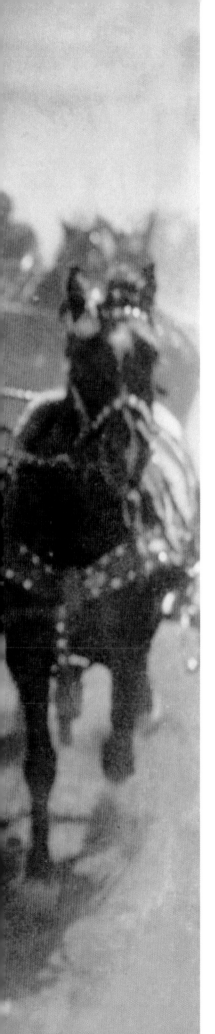

1925. The famed chariot race from *Ben-Hur*, with Ramon Novarro. The delays and reorganization had pushed the budget over $4 million. But when the movie opened in December 1925, it was such a sensation that its real loss was outweighed by the attention and prestige that came to Metro-Goldwyn-Mayer.

1925. While Mayer was on his European trip scouting out Swedish stars, he halted filming of *Ben-Hur* in Rome and ordered the production back to California. Here, in the flats of Culver City, you can see plans for the chariot race.

1926. Comedian Harold Lloyd earned a fortune from his Hal Roach films, much of which was invested in Los Angeles real estate. Here he struggles to stay on a tram in *For Heaven's Sake*.

1920s. Harry Langdon had a dreamy persona, that of an innocent simpleton, and his early success was probably exploited by his young director, the up-and-coming Frank Capra. But in 1925–6, with *Tramp Tramp Tramp*, *The Strong Man*, and *Long Pants*, Langdon gained a large following.

1920s. Is this a beautiful or a tragic face? The answer is that a great comedian can inspire both affection and sorrow at the same time. In the late 1920s, Buster Keaton was a master, married to film star Natalie Talmadge, with a huge following A few years later, he was a drunk on the slide.

1927. A slower transportation, but just as sublime: Metro's superb comedian, Buster Keaton, in *The General*, a story of trains in the days of the Civil War, much of it filmed in Oregon.

1924. In *Sherlock Jr.,* Buster played a theater projectionist who walks into his own screen and joins in its drama. It was part of Keaton's genius to see that metaphor so early and to find a way of making it work.

1928. The "Buster" had something to do with how often he was hurt while filming. Keaton loved to create elaborate physical disasters or accidents. On screen he survived as if by magic, but sometimes there was real damage on set. Here is a moment of suspended risk from *Steamboat Bill Jr.*

1923. The Western began very early, with some heroes of the real thing watching over the movie recreations. *The Covered Wagon (left)*, directed by James Cruze, was one of the first epics.

1925. William S. Hart was never a cowboy. He was a Shakespearean actor who loved and read about the West, and who became a moral stalwart in the saddle. In this off-set shot from the film *Tumbleweeds (above)*, he listens to director King Baggot.

1918. Hart directed many of his own pictures, including *The Tiger Man*, with Jane Novak *(right)*. In the film, Hart plays an outlaw who comes upon a lost wagon train in the wilderness and becomes obsessed with Novak, one of the stranded travelers and a missionary's wife.

1927. Just as Hart was slow, earnest, and seemed to have ridden a day in the dust, so Tom Mix was a thrilling showman. This desperate moment from *The Broncho Twister (left)* shows Mix's full commitment to action.

1920s. Mix was spectacular, a delighted show-off who had done some rodeo riding *(right)*. He went from Wild West shows to the movies, and was no more famous than his devoted horse, Tony.

1927. Director Frank Borzage was making a reputation for romances and women's films at the Fox studio. Here *(left)* are the 1920s' screen team Charles Farrell and Janet Gaynor as a tormented sewer cleaner and his melancholy girl in Borzage's *7th Heaven,* one of Hollywood's first bona fide tearjerkers.

1927. What happened next? That old question drove so many movies. *Body and Soul (right),* directed by Reginald Barker, may stand for the legions of lost or forgotten melodramas. But this one starred two important players—Lionel Barrymore and Aileen Pringle. As you can see, sex and violence have a history together.

1927. One of the best young directors was the lofty, artistic Josef von Sternberg. He began as a realist, but soon turned into a visionary of noir scenes with glamorous women. This still *(left)* features Evelyn Brent (as "Feathers") in a scene from *Underworld,* a gangster film without the sound of gunfire.

1928. Borzage and Gaynor seen with the new man in town—a guy named Oscar *(right),* promoted by the Academy of Motion Picture Arts and Sciences, which also aimed to out-negotiate the new unions and run public relations for the picture business. In the first year of the Oscars, Borzage and Gaynor both won for *7th Heaven*.

1928. The first Oscar for Best Picture went to Paramount for William Wellman's *Wings*, an expensive and spectacular story of air warfare during the Great War. Its stars were Buddy Rogers, Richard Arlen, and Gary Cooper *(left).*

1927. Clara Bow *(right)* was the star of *Wings*—she played a girl who was loved by the two male leads—but the movie worked because of the flying scenes. Director William Wellman was a veteran pilot, having flown with the Lafayette Escadrille—a group of elite American flying aces based in France in the First World War.

1927. There were doubts in the industry about the choice for Best Picture of 1927. *Wings* was the popular hit, but many felt a prestige award should go to *Sunrise (right),* the work of German Director, F. W. Murnau. *Sunrise* had a visionary feeling for atmosphere, lighting, and camera movement that would change the American movie—so the arty crowd voted for it.

1927. *Sunrise* starred George O'Brien as a rural farmer who is encouraged by his mistress, a city vixen, to get rid of his beloved wife, played by Janet Gaynor. Here *(left)* O'Brien and Gaynor visit the city, which leads to his character's disenchantment with the country life.

1928. One sign of the new expressive direction in American film was King Vidor's *The Crowd,* made at Metro-Goldwyn-Mayer, about nothing less than the plight of the small man in mass society. James Murray *(right)* plays the faceless worker lost in the crowd.

1927. The film that changed everything was *The Jazz Singer (right),* a Warner Brothers production that banked everything on the revolution of seeing moving images and hearing speech at the same time. In this still Al Jolson turns to his mother and is about to take advantage of synchronized sound.

1920s. At the end of an era, the movies were still about faces. And some faces knew how to be photographed—or the camera loved them. Clara Bow *(left),* who had starred with Gary Cooper in *Wings,* had been the "It" girl, a wow and a sensation in films like *It* and *Hula.* But sound would wipe her out at the age of 23.

1929. The new era of sound films seemed made for the tense pauses that marked Gary Cooper (in one of his last silent films, *Betrayal, right*) as an actor of the new age.

1930s

1939. At the end of the 1930s, Hollywood made several movies (rich in the new Technicolor) that would represent the American movie for decades to come. Maybe longer. One of them was *The Wizard of Oz (right)*, an extraordinary merger of childhood material with adult hopes and fears.

1930s

The Studio System

1930s. The early sound stage was a battleground *(left)*. The noisy camera had a cubicle of its own. Microphones were everywhere, and the actors had to stay close to them. As a result, the action in movies froze. But these problems were solved, and soon fluidity came back to enhance the naturalism of talk, sound effects, and the real novelty: quiet actors, thinking silently. It is almost impossible to be quiet for long in a silent film.

1935. Astaire and Rogers *(previous pages)* exemplified a world of black-and-white glamour. Fred and Ginger played characters in a high society world where sets and clothes smacked of money and vanity fair. Economically, America was doing less well–but escapism through cinema was on its way to becoming the leading form of American entertainment. Here are the song-and-dance team nonpareil in *Top Hat,* dancing "Cheek to Cheek."

In the 1930s, America—and the world—faced tough and disturbing times. The lasting effects of the great crash of 1929 and the rise of fascist governments put more pressure on the American dream than at any time since the Civil War.

It was hard for movie studios, too. The crash came on the heels of large investments to convert stages and theaters to sound. But audiences fell off. Some could not afford the ticket price; others lacked the English to keep up with talking pictures.

Yet we look back on the 1930s as an era of movie glory. Sound brought fresh realism, narrative speed, crackling dialogue, the thrill of gunfire, and the magic of musical accompaniment. It ushered in new writers and directors and a generation of great stars— Marlene Dietrich, Gary Cooper, James Cagney, Cary Grant, Katharine Hepburn, Joan Crawford, Bette Davis, Spencer Tracy, Clark Gable, Errol Flynn, and Shirley Temple.

There were new genres: the verbal comedy of the Marx Brothers; Mae West and W. C. Fields took over from the mimes. Horror, the gangster picture, and the screwball comedy all came to life. The age went from Boris Karloff in *Frankenstein* to Gable and Vivien Leigh in *Gone with the Wind,* with room for the Busby Berkeley fantasies, the first features from Walt Disney, and the Fred Astaire–Ginger Rogers musicals. It was the time of *King Kong, Top Hat, Mr. Deeds Goes to Town, Mutiny on the Bounty,* and *Stagecoach.*

Above all, it was the dynasty of great studios (Metro-Goldwyn-Mayer, Paramount, Warners, Fox, Universal, Columbia, RKO), where everyone was hired in on seven-year contracts and most of America was thinking of ways to get to Hollywood.

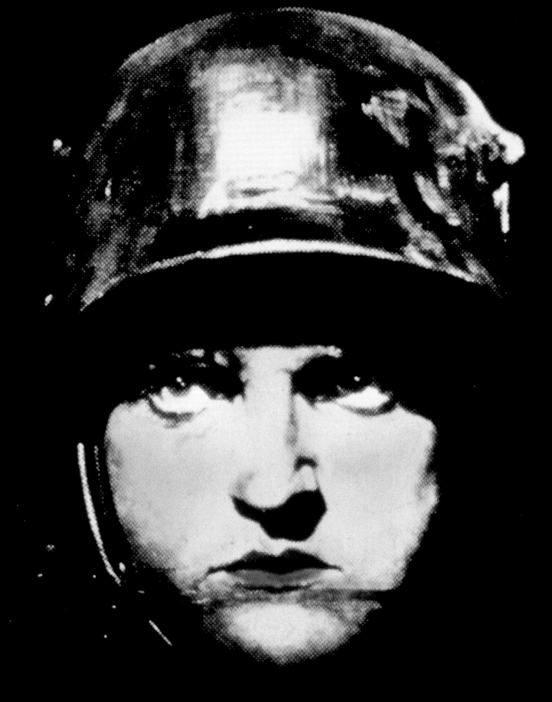

ALL QUIET
ON THE
WESTERN FRONT

1930. Adapted from the
internationally best-selling World
War I novel by Erich Maria
Remarque, *All Quiet on the
Western Front* was an intellectual
event and proof that the movies
could take on the great issues of
the time (instead of being mere
entertainment).

1930. *All Quiet on the* **Western
Front** was an early epic of sound
cinema—in which American
actors (like Lew Ayres, *center*)
played young German soldiers
in a war that had afflicted all
nations. It won Best Picture for
1929–30, and Best Director for
Lewis Milestone.

1933. In the early 1930s, talk and situations could be very daring—until the Production Code of 1934 (a self-regulatory code of ethics enacted by the major studios, prohibiting the screening of films containing material deemed "unmoral"). Here is *Baby Face (above)*, produced during the last year of liberty, in which Barbara Stanwyck sleeps her way through a New York business organization. The strictly enforced Production Code would remain in place for three more decades.

1931. Director Rouben Mamoulian proved to be highly skilled with early sound—he kept the camera moving and employed a mix of music and sound effects. His *City Streets (right)*, starring Gary Cooper and Sylvia Sidney as two lovers entangled in the gangster lifestyle, was studied and imitated by other filmmakers.

1931. The 1930s was a great age for child actors. Jackie Cooper (then only ten) played the son of a down-and-out boxer portrayed by Wallace Beery *(left)* in *The Champ*, directed by King Vidor. The same actors would play Long John Silver and Jim Hawkins in *Treasure Island* (1934).

1934. Few films showed more flesh than the Tarzan series. The man of the jungle had been a fixture of silent cinema, but the character gained sexual energy and voice with the casting of Olympic champion swimmer, Johnny Weissmuller *(left)*, seen here with Maureen O'Sullivan as Jane in *Tarzan and His Mate*.

1932. Cecil B. DeMille continued to explore ancient world decadence with his epic *The Sign of the Cross*, about early Christians persecuted by Nero. This racy scene *(right)* shows Claudette Colbert as the wicked Empress Poppaea in her bath. DeMille insisted on filling the pool with goat's milk, filled to nipple-height—but it turned to cheese under the studio lights. Charles Laughton played Nero, and Fredric March was the virtuous Roman officer.

1934. Challenging Caesar (Warren William) to notice her exposed leg, Colbert burns up the screen again as *Cleopatra (left)*, in DeMille's spectacular version of the perennially favorite Hollywood tale.

1937. Many Hollywood productions took advantage of British studios and actors. *King Solomon's Mines* was directed by Robert Stevenson (decades later he would do *Mary Poppins*). The white hunters were played by Cedric Hardwicke, Roland Young, and John Loder; and Paul Robeson—relaxing here off set— played the noble African guide.

1936. Paul Robeson sang "Ol' Man River" to powerful effect in the movie version of Jerome Kern and Oscar Hammerstein II's *Show Boat* (directed by none other than *Frankenstein*'s James Whale). The gifted Robeson was one of the most sought-after black singers and actors in the 1930s, at a time when black performers in Hollywood films were limited to stereotypical roles such as servants, comics, and bystanders.

1930s

1931. In *City Lights*, the tramp loves a beautiful blind girl (Virginia Cherrill) *(right)* in the most exquisite and wistful romance Charlie Chaplin ever handled.

1931. Charlie Chaplin was so secure that he could ignore sound. *City Lights* had music, but no dialogue. Still, for many, it is his greatest film. In this still *(left)* the tramp makes friends with a drunken rich man in an image that foreshadows film noir.

1931. At the end of *City Lights*, the blind girl can see again, but she does not notice the tramp who did so much for her. The final bittersweet close-up *(right)* is the peak of Chaplin's emotional attitude to life. A millionaire by then, he had idealistic sympathy for poor people—enough to make ignorant watchdogs accuse him of being a communist.

1930s

1930. Sound was great for gunfire, screams, and snarling voices—hence the genesis of the gangster film in the early 1930s. It also gave work to stage actors, like Edward G. Robinson. Here he is in *Little Caesar*, a classic of the new genre.

1930s

1931. The gangster film had many comic variants. *Smart Money* stars Edward G. Robinson as a gambling barber who gets even with the hustlers who scammed him, and James Cagney plays his sidekick.

1932. Director Howard Hawks and writer Ben Hecht wanted to show the private life of a gangster—the result was *Scarface*, with Paul Muni as Tony Camonte, seen here with Karen Morley and George Raft (seated). The film was subtitled *Shame of a Nation*, but everyone was having fun.

1932. Hollywood gangsters seldom ended up in prison—incarceration was reserved for cases of wrongful conviction. Paul Muni is the falsely accused veteran (with Edward Ellis) in *I Am a Fugitive from a Chain Gang*, directed by Mervyn Le Roy, an unblinkingly pessimistic picture.

1931. No gangster was as vivid, violent, or enchanting as James Cagney. Here he is in William Wellman's *The Public Enemy*, with Mae Clarke, in the film that changed America's breakfast habits and boosted the grapefruit business.

ANGELS WITH DIRTY FACES

JAMES **CAGNEY** AND PAT **O'BRIEN**

The "DEAD END" KIDS · *Humphrey* **BOGART**

ANN SHERIDAN · GEORGE BANCROFT · *Directed by* MICHAEL CURTIZ · *Presented by* **WARNER BROS.**

1933. James Cagney was a force of nature, and his energy could rub out enemies or build a great show. He was also trained as a dancer, and in *Footlight Parade (left)*, he sings and dances and steals the show as the intrepid Broadway producer who orders the showgirls around. The film, directed by Lloyd Bacon, was one of Warner's best musical extravaganzas, thanks to Busby Berkeley's brilliant choreography.

1938. At Warners, the gangster film was still a staple in the late 1930s. In *Angels with Dirty Faces (above)*, Cagney is persuaded to break down in false cowardice at the electric chair by priest Pat O'Brien, to deter the neighborhood kids from following his path. The "kids" were the Dead End Kids, who were featured in six films. By the 1940s they had evolved into the Bowery Boys (although they were well into their 30s).

1933. Warner Brothers loved to use Cagney in movies that were as fresh as the latest craze. *Picture Snatcher (left)* cast him as a current novelty—the news photographer who will do anything for a shot. What does anything mean? Look at Cagney's eyes.

1930s

1933. Groucho Marx and Margaret Dumont are not just one of the supreme comic mismatches in movie history—they make an enduringly forlorn love story as she dreams of refinement while he surrounds her with double entendres. Here they are in *Duck Soup*.

1935. The Marx brothers made four films at Paramount (from *The Cocoanuts* to *Duck Soup*). Then they were lured away to MGM, where they were given stronger love interests and songs—in an effort to tame them. This is *A Night at the Opera*, directed by the versatile Sam Wood.

1933. Mae West established her own genre, and she took full advantage of the liberated pre-Code atmosphere. As both a writer and player, West loved double or even triple meanings and sex in the head—always the most fertile place. In one of her best films, *I'm No Angel (left)*, she is the sexy sideshow performer and Cary Grant is her target. West cowrote the story and most of the dialogue, including the famous line: "Oh Beulah... Peel me a grape."

1933. In many ways, Mae West dominated her movies as if she were a man. Today, it is easier to see or feel the kind of gender-shifting in her work that has made her a lasting cultural icon—a "camp" fire maybe, but still smoldering. This is West with Dewey Robinson *(right)* in *She Done Him Wrong,* which also featured Cary Grant.

1936. The odd couple is an enduring comic principle. Oliver Hardy was from Georgia; Stan Laurel came from a small town in northern England. But as Laurel and Hardy, they were the guarantee of "a fine mess"— endearing pals always getting things wrong. They made shorts and full-length features, like *Way Out West (left)*.

1934. Legendary producer David O. Selznick began at MGM as a script reader. He rose in the ranks, and went on to run Paramount and then RKO, returning to MGM (after marrying Louis B. Mayer's daughter, Irene) in 1933. Selznick's relationship with director George Cukor began at RKO, but they made many films together at MGM, including *David Copperfield (left)*. It starred Freddie Bartholomew as the boy and W. C. Fields as Mr. Micawber (after Charles Laughton had given up on the part).

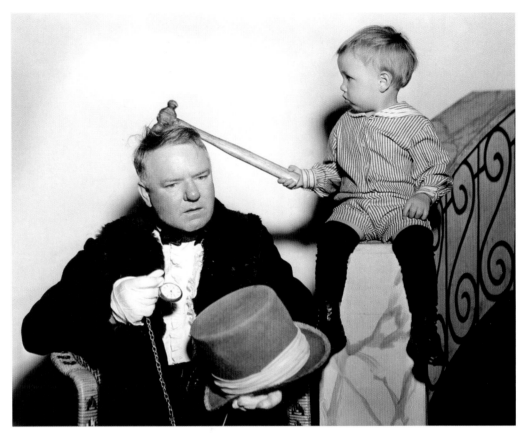

1934. W. C. Fields had been a smash hit for decades on stage. But on screen he became a comic figure like Falstaff—the sad, grumbling drunk who puts up with his wife, children, family, and all their stupid advice to be serious. Here is Fields with Baby Leroy *(right)* in *The Old-Fashioned Way*.

1935. Just a couple of Paramount players *(left):* Fields as the riverboat captain in *Mississippi*, and his sidekick—Bing Crosby—whose huge success on records and radio carried him into movies.

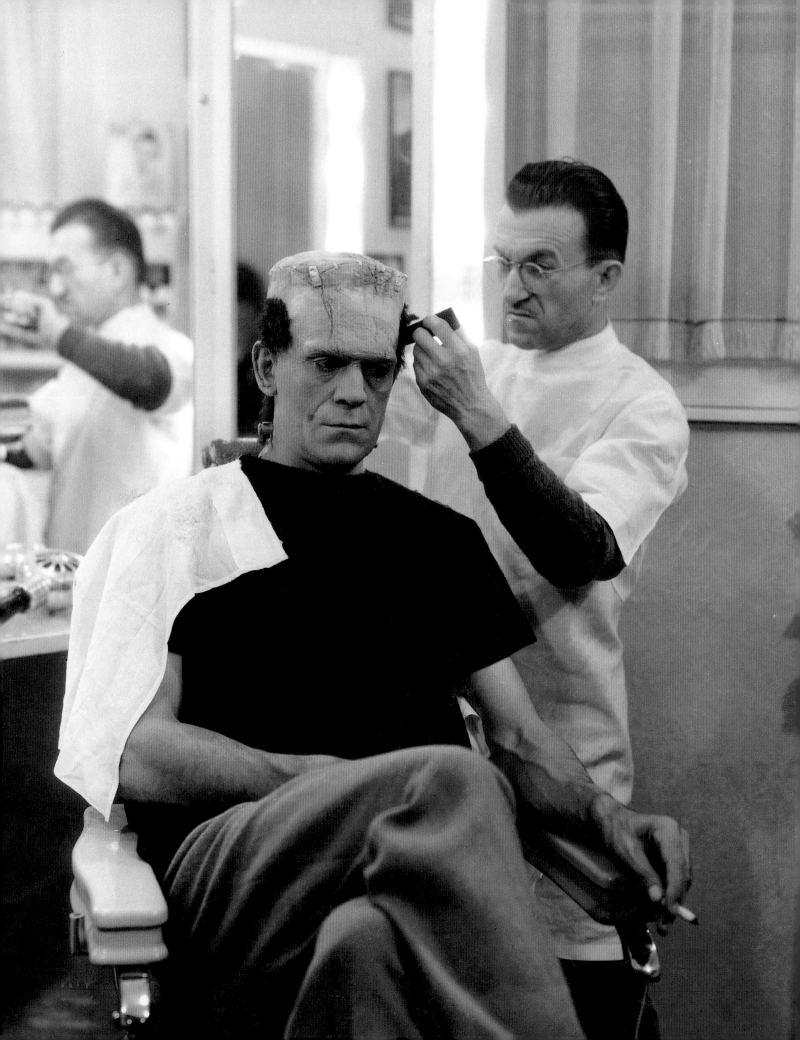

1931. Director James Whale *(above),* made the first Dracula and Frankenstein films in the sound era. Here he is on the set of *Frankenstein*, with Boris Karloff. Whale was recently portrayed by Ian McKellen in the acclaimed film *Gods and Monsters* (1998).

1931. This is one of the great scenes in horror *(right)*: the little girl and the monster, the pond and the idyllic landscape. What happens next?

1931. In movies, nothing surpasses an ambiguous face *(left):* is this one horrific or tragic? Boris Karloff was a tall, deep-voiced English actor. Transformed by makeup he became the monster in *Frankenstein*, still a disturbing and beautiful film.

1931. From *Frankenstein* to *King Kong*, there is always an underlying threat that the monster will ravish beauty. Yet Karloff brought a humanity to Frankenstein that deepened the story.

1935. The very pathos of Karloff's monster deserved a friend, and here she is: *The Bride of Frankenstein*—hissing, touched by electricity, dangerous, but sexy too. The actress is Elsa Lanchester (Charles Laughton's wife) and the director was James Whale again.

1930s

1932. Almost certainly, Karloff came from mixed blood—a father in British government service, and an Indian mother. Those looks made him perfect for *The Mummy (right)*, directed by Karl Freund, previously a great cameraman.

1932. In the early 1930s, Universal had cornered the market in players and directors that were best at horror. But other studios were ready to put on the frighteners. Thus, Paramount had Rouben Mamoulian make *Dr. Jekyll and Mr. Hyde* as a prestige production—and Fredric March *(left)* shared the Best Actor Oscar for his astonishing transformation (with Wallace Beery in *The Champ*).

1931. Seen today, *Dracula* *(right)* is not as good a film as *Frankenstein*, but here is Bela Lugosi as the Count, complaining to Helen Chandler about the difficulty in getting reliable help in Transylvania.

1933. At RKO, the team of Merian C. Cooper and Ernest B. Schoedsack had an idea for a story about beauty and the beast—it would be called *King Kong*. The film owes so much to the pluck, the near nakedness, and the screaming power of Fay Wray as Kong's beloved.

1933. Willis O'Brien was the genius behind many of the special effects in *King Kong*, which utilized the most cutting-edge technology of the time. Kong was actually an 18-inch high flexible model covered with rabbit fur, filmed frame-by-frame with stop-motion photography on miniature sets of the jungle and New York City. Stop-motion had existed for over a decade, but the Kong crew combined it with other techniques— such as rear projection, miniature projection, and blue screen—that allowed the actors and King Kong to share the screen in a way audiences had never seen before.

1931. Director Josef von Sternberg and actress Marlene Dietrich *(left)* pose in a publicity shot. Born Maria Magdalene Dietrich, the young actress was a minor German figure when Von Sternberg found her in 1930 and cast her as the lead in *The Blue Angel (Der blaue Engel)*. The film's worldwide success made Dietrich a star, and Von brought her back to America to sign with Paramount. Though married to others, they were lovers while making another six immortal pictures together.

1930. *Morocco* was Dietrich's first American film. Here is Dietrich's character *(above)*, a sultry cabaret singer, with the other man in her life, played by Adolphe Menjou. Von Sternberg took a fatalistic relish in casting actors who resembled him and usually represented a man humiliated in love.

1930. It was in *Morocco,* and then in life, that Dietrich *(left)* popularized such things as pants on women, smoking as a sexual metaphor, and an eye for the ladies (as well as the men). This style was the more suggestive in that it was never explained or spelled out in the movies.

1932. In *Blonde Venus,* Dietrich *(right)* plays a nightclub singer who is also a devoted mother. Von Sternberg used décor and light to convey story and mood, but this is 1932 when the sexual metaphor of the openmouthed mask was bolder.

1932. In *Shanghai Express,* Dietrich is the infamous Shanghai Lily, who encounters her old flame, English actor Clive Brook *(left)*, and a lot of trouble in first class on the train from Peiping, China, to Shanghai. Von Sternberg uses shadow as a net in which characters seem trapped. Lee Grames, who also worked with von Sternberg on Morocco, won the Oscar for Best Cinematography.

1935. Dietrich plays the heartless femme fatale Concha Perez *(right)* in her last project with von Sternberg—*The Devil is a Woman,* the most sardonic and cruel of their seven collaborations. In this film, an older man who is obsessed with Dietrich recounts his heartbreak to a younger man who is in the process of becoming similarly ensnared. In this mid-1930s work, cinema reached a peak in the portrayal of adult relationships not yet surpassed.

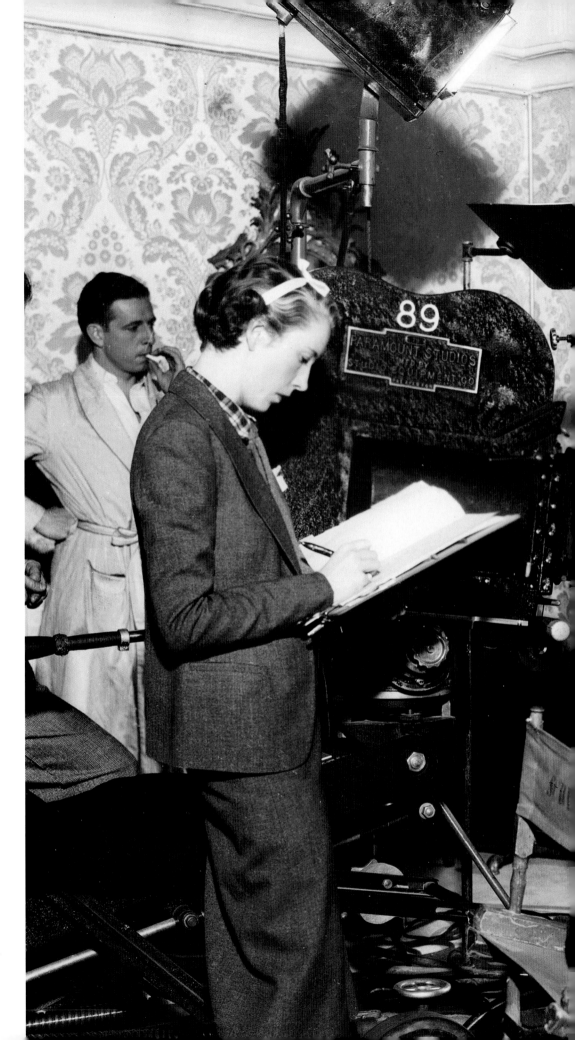

1930s

1937. There was a circle of very creative Germans in Hollywood: here is Ernst Lubitsch directing Marlene Dietrich in *Angel* (with sets by Hans Dreier and music by Friedrich Hollander). In 1946 Lubitsch won a special Oscar for his 32 years in movies.

1932. Sure, international stars had an aura of intrigue, but don't forget the American beauties. Lucille Fay Le Sueur was born in San Antonio, Texas. No one worked harder to be a star—to be Joan Crawford, seen here in *Letty Lynton (left)*.

1938. Art copied life: in many of her best films Joan started at the bottom, lost her pride and other things along the way, but battled to the top. In this still *(right)*, she is an ordinary shop girl punching a time clock in Frank Borzage's *Mannequin*.

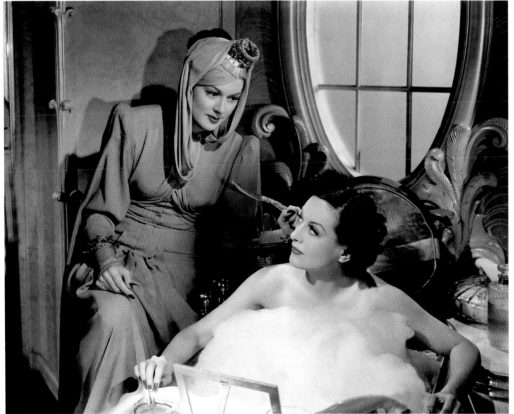

1939. After two years of testing Scarletts, George Cukor was fired from *Gone With the Wind*. Metro snapped him up to direct *The Women*. Adapted by Anita Loos and Jane Murfin from Claire Booth's Broadway play, the women in *The Women* have a great time trying to outdo each other for richer men, flashier wardrobes, and juicier gossip. The casting exploited the real-life rivalry between Norma Shearer and Joan Crawford. Crawford plays a shopgirl (seen here with Rosalind Russell, *left*) who tries to steal Shearer's husband.

1939. George Cukor poses with the ensemble cast of *The Women, from left to right:* Florence Nash, Phyllis Povah, Rosalind Russell, Joan Crawford, Cukor, Norma Shearer, Paulette Goddard, Mary Boland, and Joan Fontaine.

1935. Bette Davis used her real name, more or less (she was born Ruth Elizabeth Davis, in Lowell Massachusetts); she trained for the stage; and she was the queen of the Warner Brothers lot. *Dangerous* was a routine film about a jinxed alcoholic actress rehabilitated by love, but it won her the first of two Oscars.

1937. Bette felt that Warners should be giving her better parts; when they didn't, she went to London to make a picture out of contract. Although Warners won the ensuing court case, Bette ended up with the parts she wanted. In *Marked Woman (right)*, she's a prostitute and Humphrey Bogart is the D.A. (based on the real-life Thomas Dewey), trying to get her to testify against the Mob.

1939. *Dark Victory* was one of Bette's great melodramas—a terminally ill heiress *(left)* begins to lose her vision and fall in love at the same time—and got her a nomination for best actress (she lost to Vivien Leigh's Scarlett). But you can see where the idea came from for "Bette Davis Eyes," the 1981 Kim Carnes song.

1938. *Jezebel* was Warners' effort to persuade David Selznick that Bette *(right)* should play Scarlett O'Hara (and why not with Errol Flynn as Rhett Butler?) Selznick was unmoved, but the Academy voted Bette her second Oscar, and she forged a bond with director William Wyler.

1930s. Garbo was a favorite subject for the great still photographers *(left)* and an expert at showing her beauty and her reticence at the same time. This was consistent with her whole career, in which she always seemed to flinch from fame. Thus, she spent her last six decades as a legend, to be seen in Manhattan sometimes, but never in new movies.

1932. Throughout the 1930s, MGM had the best record, the most stars, and some terrific pictures. *Grand Hotel (above)*, directed by Edmund Goulding and master-minded by Irving Thalberg, was an all-star enterprise, with Greta Garbo as an egocentric prima ballerina.

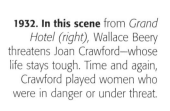

1932. In this scene from *Grand Hotel (right)*, Wallace Beery threatens Joan Crawford—whose life stays tough. Time and again, Crawford played women who were in danger or under threat.

1939. Garbo had a deep, accented voice that she could use with great feeling. But more profoundly, she was a grave and external face, adored by the camera. Here *(above),* she is on the set of *Queen Christina,* rehearsing one of the most famous moments in her career.

1939. Ernst Lubitsch's sound films at Paramount added to his reputation for the "Lubitsch touch," and he had a brief stint as production chief at the studio. But then he moved over to Metro and made Garbo laugh in *Ninotchka (right),* a film written by Walter Reisch, Charles Brackett, and Billy Wilder.

1933. The ending of *Queen Christina,* with Garbo sailing away *(left),* abdicating her throne for love. Keep your face blank, Mamoulian told her. The audience will supply your thoughts.

1936. Rash ambition or masterpiece? Shortly before his death, Thalberg insisted on casting his wife, Norma Shearer, in *Romeo and Juliet*, with Leslie Howard. Norma was 35, Leslie was 42. George Cukor directed but he couldn't hide those facts of life.

1936. Spencer Tracy had a fine on-screen rapport with that other Metro giant, Clark Gable. In *San Francisco (left)*, Gable plays a racy club owner who falls in love with a chaste singer (Jeanette MacDonald) over the objections of his friend, Father Tim. The film also included footage of the Great 1906 Earthquake.

1938. Two years later, Tracy played a priest again, Father Flanagan, who stands up for Mickey Rooney in the inspirational (and pretty sentimental) *Boys Town (right)*.

1936. Fritz Lang, fleeing Nazi Germany, also ended up at Metro, where he made *Fury (right)*, a stark indictment of lynch law. Spencer Tracy played the man nearly killed by the mob, and vowing vengeance. Tracy is seen here with love interest Sylvia Sidney.

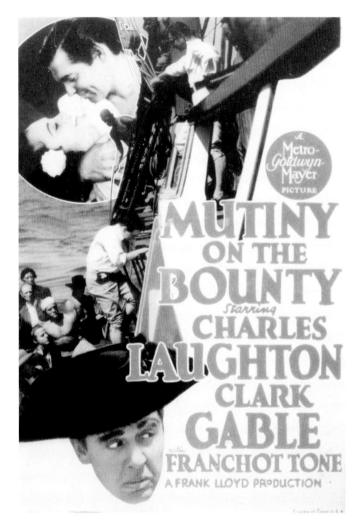

1936. Mutiny on the Bounty was one of the last big productions supervised personally by Irving Thalberg. An epic story of cruel authority and revenge, it defined the action picture that also contains psychological conflict.

1936. In the film, Clark Gable leads the uprising against the vicious Captain Bligh (Charles Laughton), seen here with veteran actor, Donald Crisp. *Mutiny on the Bounty* won the Oscar for Best Picture, although it was nominated for eight awards, including three Best Actor nominations—Clark Gable, Charles Laughton, and Franchot Tone—the only time three actors from the same film have been nominated. Victor McLaglen actually won the Oscar, for *The Informer*.

1938. MGM created the singing team of Nelson Eddy and Jeanette MacDonald, adored as America's "singing sweethearts" in the 1930s, seen here in *The Girl of the Golden West (left)*.

ROBERT DONAT
THE BEST PICTURE OF ANY YEAR·
GOODBYE MR. CHIPS
with **GREER GARSON**

A **SAM WOOD** PRODUCTION
Screen Play by R. C. SHERRIFF,
CLAUDINE WEST and ERIC MASCHWITZ
Produced by VICTOR SAVILLE

A Metro-Goldwyn-Mayer PICTURE

1939. Another find for MGM was Greer Garson, who costarred with Robert Donat in Sam Wood's *Goodbye, Mr. Chips (right)*, based on the James Hilton novel about the life of a British schoolteacher.

1939. Although Donat had played the lead in Hitchcock's *39 Steps,* his endearing portrayal of of the gentle Mr. Chips *(left)* made him a star. Donat actually stole the Oscar away from Clark Gable and Rhett Butler.

1934. Elsewhere in Hollywood, the 1930s saw the rise of Sicilian-born Frank Capra. He had begun in silent comedy, and then found a home at Columbia Pictures. Here he is with his favorite cameraman, Joseph Walker, working on *It Happened One Night*.

1934. *It Happened One Night* was a smart comedy of talk and manners. Starring Clark Gable and Claudette Colbert, it won Oscars for Best Picture, best director, for Gable and Colbert, and for screenwriter Robert Riskin.

1939. Many of Capra's films were rooted in the Depression and the sense of national recovery. They concerned folk heroes who could reanimate the American spirit and reform corrupt government, as in *Mr. Smith Goes to Washington,* which pitted James Stewart against Claude Rains.

1936. Gary Cooper (seen here with Jean Arthur) portrays another Capra champion in *Mr. Deeds Goes to Town*—a rural poet inherits a fortune and plans to give it all away to struggling farmers, much to the consternation of money-hungry city estate lawyers.

1930s

1933. Katharine Hepburn was one of the more controversial stars of the 1930s. There was no doubt about her ability—she won an Oscar for *Morning Glory* (1933)—but was she also box-office poison? In *Christopher Strong*, she plays an Amelia Earhart-like aviatrix, directed by Dorothy Arzner—the only woman director of the age.

1937. Technicolor was the painterly system first introduced in the mid-1930s with Rouben Mamoulian's *Becky Sharp*. Mamoulian (seated, in the center) is seen here on set directing Miriam Hopkins in the film, a retelling of the William Thackeray novel *Vanity Fair*.

1937. *Dead End* **was** an important film for legendary producer Sam Goldwyn, in which his top director (William Wyler) took on the problem of the slums. Wyler (far right) directs Joel McCrea, Allen Jenkins, and Humphrey Bogart—playing the villain. The young Bowery Boys rounded out the cast.

1935. What secrets does a St. Bernard keep? Here are Loretta Young and Clark Gable in William Wellman's *Call of the Wild*. It was after this location shoot that Young found herself pregnant— with a daughter who looked a lot like Gable.

1933. The black-and-white musical was hugely popular with Warner Brothers specializing in the genre. *42nd Street (above)* was directed by Lloyd Bacon, and starred Dick Powell, Ruby Keeler, and Bebe Daniels. Its greatest asset was the big dance numbers, by Busby Berkeley.

1933. Berkeley relaxes *(left)* on the set of *Gold Diggers,* directed by Mervyn LeRoy. Berkeley was a choreographer who loved huge sets, geometric form, and high-angle shots. In the 1930s and 1940s, he was behind some of the biggest, sexiest, and most surreal numbers.

1933. *Footlight Parade* *(right),* showing one of Berkeley's classic overhead compositions. The only other director getting such effects in the 1930s was Leni Riefenstahl in Germany—and her subjects were Nazi storm troopers!i

FRED ASTAIRE ★★★★★ GINGER ROGERS

The king and queen of rhythm on a joyous jamboree!

"TOP HAT"

with
EDWARD EVERETT HORTON
HELEN BRODERICK
ERIK RHODES
ERIC BLORE

Directed by Mark Sandrich
RKO-RADIO PICTURE
A PANDRO S. BERMAN PRODUCTION

See Them Dance The "Piccolino!"...Hear The Songs You Can't Forget!

Lyrics and Music by IRVING BERLIN

1935. It's Frederick Austerlitz and Ginny McMath—a.k.a. Fred and Ginger—in a poster for *Top Hat (above)*, the fourth of ten films the charismatic musical duo made together. Set to a popular Irving Berlin score, it is considered one of their best films.

1936. Fred had danced on stage with his sister, Adele; Ginger had been a salty comic actress. But they came together on the sound stages of RKO and clicked. He gave her class; she lent him sex. It started with *Flying Down to Rio* (1933), and the grace has never been surpassed. Here are Fred and Ginger in *Swing Time (right)*, dancing to "Pick Yourself Up."

1935. They made it all seem so easy or natural *(far right)*: director Mark Sandrich; Ginger; Fred; and composer Irving Berlin relax during the making of *Top Hat.*

1930s

1930. Sophisticated comedy is one of the goldmines of Hollywood in the 1930s. It's a genre where many films still wait to be discovered by today's audience, like *Laughter,* directed by Harry d'Abbadie d'Arrast, starring Nancy Carroll and Fredric March.

1934. In Dashiell Hammett's novel, the thin man was the murder victim. But in Metro's hugely popular movie series, it was William Powell who was *The Thin Man,* Nick Charles. With his wife, Nora (Myrna Loy), and their dog Asta, he solved crimes, swapped drinks and wisecracks, and stayed married in six films. In this off-set shot, Powell and Loy pose with Asta.

1937. In comedies of remarriage, a divorcing couple realize—but is it too late?—how much they really love each other. Leo McCarey's *The Awful Truth* is a classic example of this form of screwball, and a showcase for the acting of Irene Dunne and Cary Grant.

1932. Ernst Lubitsch gave the screwball genre a helping hand with *Trouble in Paradise*, in which all the lovers tell lies. Here are Herbert Marshall and Miriam Hopkins in the war of the loving sexes.

GRETA GARBO'S TRUE LIFE STORY

ModernScreen

1938

JANUARY
10
CENTS

THE LARGEST
CIRCULATION
OF ANY SCREEN
MAGAZINE

Earl Christy

KATHARINE
HEPBURN

1938. Katharine Hepburn on the cover of *Modern Screen (left).* She was a star from the outset, and she won her first Oscar in 1932 with *Morning Glory.* But she suffered at the box office for seeming so smart and classy.

1938. A screwball of near-madness: it's Cary Grant again with Katharine Hepburn *(above)* in Howard Hawks's superb *Bringing Up Baby,* in which the provinces of Connecticut begin to seem like a jungle.

1935. An unusual portrait shot of Hepburn that suggests her androgynous quality *(right).* In George Cukor's *Sylvia Scarlett* she went disguised as a boy—and the film was a huge flop.

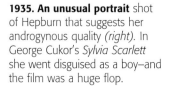

1930s

1939. *Only Angels Have Wings* seems to be an adventure film, with guys flying the mail through tricky Andean passes. But it was all done on the Columbia lot and it actually plays like screwball. Why not, with Hawks directing Cary Grant, seen here with Thomas Mitchell and Jean Arthur *(right)*.

1936. Sometimes screwball and social satire overlapped, as in *My Man Godfrey (left)*, where the action begins with a society scavenger hunt, searching skid row for a homeless or "forgotten" man. Carole Lombard is the rich girl who finds down-and-out William Powell, hires him as the family butler, and falls in love with him. The film was directed by Gregory La Cava. Here we see Powell serving Alice Brady, the family matriarch.

1939. In many other years, *Midnight* would have been famous as a comic masterpiece. But 1939 was such a rich year. In this scene *(right)* Claudette Colbert tries to work her wiles on Francis Lederer (playing a rich gigolo) while John Barrymore looks on. Don Ameche also starred as the taxi driver hopelessly in love with Colbert. The film was directed by Mitchell Leisen and written by Charles Brackett and Billy Wilder.

1932. A Hollywood story:
Harlean Carpenter was born in
Kansas City in 1911. She eloped
to Los Angeles and soon found
herself in pictures as a very sexy
platinum blonde, Jean Harlow—
seen here *(left)* with Clark Gable
in Victor Fleming's *Red Dust.* She
became an icon.

1932. In 1932, Harlow married
the MGM executive, Paul Bern
(left), who had taken her under
his wing. After two months of
marriage, during the filming of
Red Dust, Bern was dead—a
suicide after sexual failure? Or
killed by a prior wife?

1933. Harlow survived the Bern
scandal and made several more
pictures. But she was dead
herself in 1937 from kidney
disease. She remains one of
Hollywood's all-time sex
goddesses, not least for her
ability, as in this studio portrait
(above), to personify sexual
availability. It was the legend that
she wore no underwear and had
no illusions.

1930s–1940s. David O. Selznick was not the only independent producer to stand up against the studio system in the 1930s. The other rebel was Sam Goldwyn *(right)*, born Shmuel Gelbfisz in Poland, the son of a used-furniture dealer. After starting a production company in New York (it eventually became Paramount), he founded a Hollywood company that was merged into Metro-Goldwyn-Mayer. Goldwyn left his revised name in MGM, but by the late 1920s he had his own set-up.

1934. In *Twentieth Century* (directed by Howard Hawks), the struggle of wits is ingeniously sustained on a train going across the country. Hawks *(above)* is chatting with his two stars—Carole Lombard and John Barrymore, over 50 now, but still handsome.

1934. A big player in the Hollywood studios, Darryl F. Zanuck was born poor in Wahoo, Nebraska. He fought in World War I at 15, wrote screenplays for Thalberg and Sennett in his late teens, and was Warners's head of production at 23. Zanuck quit to form Twentieth Century Pictures in 1933; two years later he bought Fox, creating the colossus 20th Century Fox. Zanuck, holding a top hat, is seen here *(right)* with George Arliss at the premiere of his *House of Rothschild*.

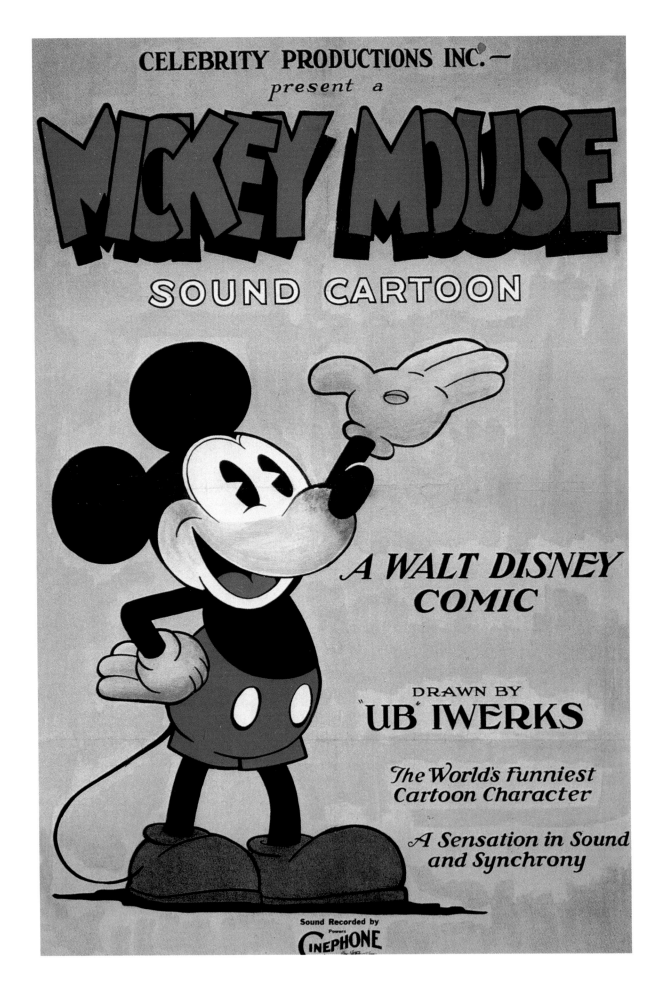

1930s. Walt Disney was an art student at the Kansas City Art Institute in the late 1910s. He moved to Los Angeles in 1923, hired some of his fellow students as animators, got financial backing from his brother and a Hollywood distributor, and founded a successful animation studio. When the distributor stole his new character Oswald the Rabbit, Disney and his sidekick Ub Iwerks struck back with their creation, a mouse named Mickey. *Steamboat Willie* (1928) was the first synchronized sound cartoon and Mickey Mouse was, and is, an unstoppable success. This poster *(left)* advertises one of the early Mickey movies from the 1930s.

1937. Disney continued his success with various animated characters through the 1930s. In 1937 he tried something new: a feature-length animated film. *Snow White and the Seven Dwarfs (above)* was an artistic masterpiece and a financial bonanza: the public loved it, and Disney won a special honorary Oscar (plus seven miniature ones for each of the dwarves).

1935. Perhaps the most far-reaching genius in American film, Disney *(right)* is not just a pioneer of animated film. He is the source of a special attitude to merchandised fun, and an inventor who has changed our sense of childhood.

1938. At Warner Brothers, Errol Flynn was at his peak in *The Adventures of Robin Hood (left)*, a film that had the most beautiful Technicolor yet and a superb score by Erich Wolfgang Korngold. Maid Marian is played by Olivia de Havilland.

1939. Sam Goldwyn and director William Wyler went into the California Sierra to duplicate the North Yorkshire moors, to find a setting for Emily Brontë's *Wuthering Heights (right)*. Merle Oberon had the female lead and the part of Heathcliffe went to Laurence Olivier. (And what effect did that have on *Gone with the Wind*?)

1939. John Steinbeck's *Of Mice and Men* was directed by Lewis Milestone and it was notable for the acting of Burgess Meredith and Lon Chaney Jr., shown in this scene still with Betty Field.

1932. While David O. Selznick was at Metro he produced *Dinner at Eight,* like *Grand Hotel* another MGM film with an all-star cast. George Cukor directed, and the stars included, among many others, both John and Lionel Barrymore, Jean Harlow, and seen here, Marie Dressler and Madge Evans. Dressler, age 63 in 1932, was that rarity—a female star of mature years. She had won the Oscar already, in *Min and Bill,* and she regularly got top billing.

1933. *Little Women* was one of Selznick's last films at RKO, and a favorite of director George Cukor. He and Hepburn would be friends and coworkers for forty years and nine pictures. They are rehearsing here with Douglass Montgomery.

1935. Selznick produced the MGM version of Leo Tolstoy's *Anna Karenina*, directed by Clarence Brown, with Greta Garbo as Anna and Fredric March as Vronsky.

163

1935. Selznick's last film at MGM was *A Tale of Two Cities (left)*, one of the best parts Ronald Colman (seated) ever had. But Selznick had by then formed an alliance with Jock Whitney, one of the richest men in America. By 1936 he was independent, and ready to pay $50,000 for a book called *Gone with the Wind*.

1936. From the novel by Hervey Allen, *Anthony Adverse (right)* was a good example of the expensive costume drama. Fredric March plays a young man who travels through three continents searching for himself. Mervyn LeRoy directed and the cast included Olivia de Havilland, Claude Rains, and Gale Sondergaard, who won the supporting actress Oscar.

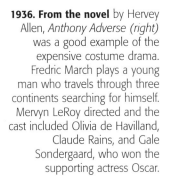

1935. It's March again in Hugo's *Les Miserables (left)*. In this version, his Jean Valjean was pursued by the Javert of Charles Laughton. (In the most recent version of the same story, it was Liam Neeson vs. Geoffrey Rush.)

1939. This still captures John Carradine, Louise Platt, and Wayne *(above)* in a moment from *Stagecoach* that shows Ford's eye for shadow and diagonals.

1939. In stressing that *Stagecoach* was the story of "nine oddly assorted strangers" (as touted on this lobby card, *right)*, Ford helped the Western be a group portrait worthy of such admirable character actors as Carradine, Thomas Mitchell, Donald Meek, and Andy Devine.

1939. 1939 was a mythical year of filmmaking in Hollywood. John Ford's contribution was *Stagecoach (left)*, maybe the first modern Western, with an all-star cast that included an actor he'd been keeping an eye on for years—John Wayne. In this off-set photograph, you can see Ford just behind Wayne's left shoulder.

1936. One of the first Selznick International pictures was *The Garden of Allah*, with Marlene Dietrich and Charles Boyer. Here *(left)* you can see the stars rehearsing by an oasis, not in north Africa, but close to Yuma, Arizona.

1936. In Metro's *The Great Ziegfeld (right)*, William Powell played impresario Florenz Ziegfeld, and Luise Rainer won the Oscar as his wife (the film also won Best Picture). Rainer won again, next year, as the Chinese peasant O-Lan in *The Good Earth*.

1936. Paul Muni was often cast as a famous figure from history. He won his Oscar as the genius chemist in *The Story of Louis Pasteur (left)*. Josephine Hutchinson played his wife.

1937. It's Janet Gaynor and the Oscar again *(right)*. But here she's receiving one in character as Vicki Lester in *A Star is Born*, the Selznick production, directed by William Wellman.

1939. Irene Dunne and Charles Boyer in *Love Affair (left)*, directed by Leo McCarey, one of the most enduring love stories. McCarey remade the story in 1957 as *An Affair to Remember*, with Cary Grant and Deborah Kerr.

1937. Sam Goldwyn hired King Vidor to direct Barbara Stanwyck in the classic woman's picture, *Stella Dallas*. In the crucial scene *(right)*, the mother (Stanwyck) is on the cold street outside watching her daughter (Anne Shirley) get married to a wealthy man.

1933. The daughter of a Santa Monica bank teller, Shirley Temple *(left)* made her first movie at the age of 4, imitating much older stars. She could sing and dance; she could do comic turns and big teary scenes. The sour English critic, Graham Greene, would say she was like a cunning adult pretending to be a child. But in the 1930s he was nearly alone in not loving Shirley.

1936. Shirley was a box-office salvation for Twentieth Century-Fox, who signed her to an exclusive contract in 1934. In 1935 she won a special Academy Award for her contribution to film (she was 7). From 1936–38, Shirley was a bigger moneymaker than Clark Gable, Gary Cooper, or Joan Crawford. In this photo *(right)*, Shirley does duty at Grauman's Chinese Theatre.

1934. The "Our Gang" series began in 1922 and ran until 1944. In other words, generations of kid actors came and went in their service. Here *(left)* we see one of the casts doing their obligatory schoolwork on the set at the Hal Roach Studios. No one ever called it a real education, but it observed the law.

1930s

1939. There were still two more classics to come in 1939. *The Wizard of Oz* made many changes to L. Frank Baum's novel; it mixed color and black and white; and endured terrible problems. But it worked, and made Judy Garland, seen here in the tornado scene *(top)* a huge star.

1939. *The Wizard of Oz* was produced by Mervyn LeRoy and Arthur Freed, and Victor Fleming directed most of it (though King Vidor shot Judy Garland singing "Over the Rainbow"). In this classic scene *(above)* Dorothy and her compatriots follow the Yellow Brick Road.

1939. The Munchkins had a famously naughty time during the making of *The Wizard of Oz*, but here the team arrange themselves for a cheerful group portrait *(right)* with LeRoy, Garland, and Fleming.

1939. *The Wizard of Oz* fleshed out the Kansas scenes in the story, and the characters Dorothy had encountered in Oz were cleverly resurrected as her dear friends and family at the film's end. *From left to right,* Frank Morgan, Judy Garland, Charley Grapewin, Ray Bolger, Jack Haley, Bert Lahr, and Clara Blandick.

1939. On the Selznick lot (the old Pathe studio in Culver City), cinematographer Ernest Haller (looking through a lens) rehearses Leigh *(left)*. Casting for Scarlett began in fall of 1936. Over the next two years hundreds of actresses were tested (including Paulette Goddard and Lana Turner); more than 28 miles of film was used for screen tests; and almost $500,000 was spent. Finally, Vivien Leigh—who had come to America to be with Laurence Olivier as he did *Wuthering Heights*, was hired on Christmas of 1938.

1939. 1939 ended with the release of another landmark movie: Selznick's *Gone with the Wind.* This still *(above)* shows Gerald O'Hara (Thomas Mitchell) with his three daughters and Mammy (Hattie McDaniel). McDaniel won the supporting actress Oscar (the first ever won by a black performer), but Selznick yielded to requests from the civic authorities of Atlanta that she not attend the film's premiere on December 15.

1939. David O. Selznick and Clark Gable share a smoke on the *Gone with the Wind* set *(left)*. Gable and some money were traded to Selznick by MGM for the right to distribute the picture. So Gable felt used. He declined to do a Southern accent and helped get George Cukor fired.

179

1939. It was a very hard shoot—
at six days a week under
Technicolor lights, in heavy
costumes. Leigh and Gable
(never too fond of each other)
listen to director Victor Fleming
(in spectacles).

1940s

1940. Yes, they're crazy about each other: Cary Grant and Rosalind Russell in Howard Hawks's *His Girl Friday (right)*, a gender adjustment of the Ben Hecht-Charles MacArthur play, *The Front Page*. In screwball comedy, when people squabble, argue and interrupt each other, they're in love.

1940s

The Dream Turns Dark

In the 1940s, perhaps, Hollywood did its greatest work. It was a vital part of the war effort, sustaining morale both at home and abroad. In the years after victory, the cinema enjoyed the largest audiences it would ever have. Hollywood also benefited from the grave new experiences that Americans had faced in Europe and the Pacific; national ideals had been tested and proved, imparting a new confidence and a feeling that America must be ready to lead the world. At the same time, the grim scenery of the war was enough to breed conscience and anxiety. Thus, as the post-war era began, film noir slipped across Hollywood screens, arguably the most adult genre the studios would ever fashion. This was also the heyday of the musical and the Western, and the moment when the last great generation of stars arrived—including Gregory Peck, William Holden, Burt Lancaster, Doris Day, Rita Hayworth, Robert Mitchum, and Marlon Brando.

However, major changes were to come: after 1947, film audiences began to decline—a process still ongoing—driven by the rise of television. TV would ultimately become larger than the movies, even if it seldom matched their majesty or beauty.

The business grew less rewarding as studios were compelled by anti-monopoly legislation to sell off their theaters and stars began to seek a percentage of film profits. From 1947 onwards, Hollywood was undermined by investigations made for the House Un-American Activities Committee. Yet despite the turmoil, this was the decade that produced such films as *Citizen Kane, Casablanca, It's a Wonderful Life, Gilda, Crossfire, Notorious*, and *The Lost Weekend*.

1949. Cecil B. DeMille was still raiding the Bible for stories in the 1940s. *Samson and Delilah (left)* is one of his best—with Victor Mature and Hedy Lamarr.

1946. Together in real life, how could you keep Bogart and Bacall apart on screen? Howard Hawks teamed them again in *The Big Sleep (previous pages)*, based on the Raymond Chandler book, and the result was part noir, part mystery, part romance, and part screwball.

1940. Set in Budapest (without reference to Nazis or war), *The Shop Around the Corner* is Ernst Lubitsch's most tender film. James Stewart and Margaret Sullavan don't get on. And they have no idea that the secret love letters they are writing go to . . . each other.

1943. *In Heaven Can Wait,* Don Ameche (seen here with Gene Tierney) plays a man in the hereafter who is rueful about his past sins and looking back on his life. But Ernst Lubitsch and his favorite writer, Samson Raphaelson, kept the delicate situation witty and filled with feeling.

1940. If 1939 was a rich year, what about 1940? Katharine Hepburn had *The Philadelphia Story* written as a stage play just for her. Then she shepherded the movie into being at Metro, with Cary Grant and James Stewart as her partners, and George Cukor directing.

1940. But the greatest luck Hepburn had in 1940 was finding Spencer Tracy in George Stevens's *Woman of the Year*. There was an unexpected chemistry. Her air of box-office "poison" vanished and Tracy became more lovable.

1940. Errol Flynn as a privateer in Elizabethan costume with sword at the ready *(left)*. *The Sea Hawk* seems to portray sixteenth century England vs. Spain, but it's a hugely entertaining parable about England vs. Hitler's Germany, encouraging the United States to join the fight. Michael Curtiz directed and Erich Wolfgang Korngold composed the powerful score.

1940. Flynn was not the only swashbuckling hero in the 1940s; at 20th Century Fox, Tyrone Power had one of his great successes in *The Mark of Zorro (right)*, directed by Rouben Mamoulian. The Zorro story, and its stereotyped view of Mexico, shows no sign of waning—but Power in the 1940s was one of those actors who truly believed in his own heroics. And today that faith is more rare.

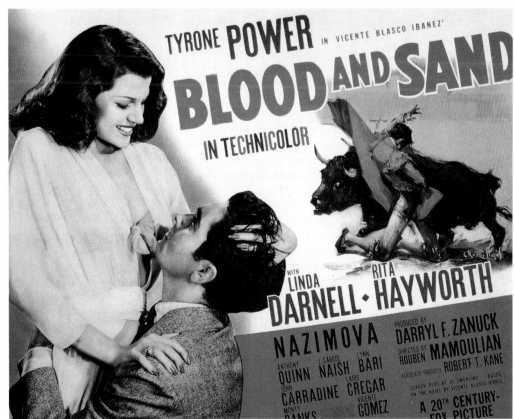

1941. Working for Mamoulian again, Power played the young bullfighter in *Blood and Sand (left)*, torn between Ms. Darnell and Rita Hayworth, formerly Carmen Cansino, and a knockout supporting player in *Only Angels Have Wings*.

1940. Encouraged by boss Darryl Zanuck, John Ford took the John Steinbeck novel, *The Grapes of Wrath*, and conveyed a searing impression of Dustbowl Depression. *From left to right,* Dorris Bowden as Rosasharn, Jane Darwell as Ma, and Henry Fonda as Tom Joad.

1941. Frank Capra's mood was growing more anxious in the early 1940s, and in *Meet John Doe* he showed how close populism and fascism could be. Gary Cooper was the harrowed folk hero, seen here with Barbara Stanwyck and James Gleason.

1941. One of the great debuts in 1941 occurred when 35-year-old screenwriter John Huston got to direct *The Maltese Falcon*. Here we see Humphrey Bogart, Peter Lorre, Mary Astor, and Sydney Greenstreet clustered around the falcon, "the stuff of dreams."

1941. It was a key year for Bogart. He was the hero in *The Maltese Falcon*, and in Raoul Walsh's *High Sierra* he was a sympathetic ex-con driven back into old ways. (The screenplay was written by John Huston and W. R. Burnett.) Bogart seemed older, wiser, sadder, more relaxed—a star at last. He is with Ida Lupino here, one of the best actresses of the 1940s.

1949. *They Live By Night* is one of the great noir movies. It was director Nicholas Ray's first film, and starred Farley Granger and Cathy O'Donnell as two young people hounded by fate.

1941. All in white, on the set of *Citizen Kane (left),* Orson Welles—the film's director, cowriter, and star—confers with Gregg Toland, the experienced cameraman who was so important to the film's innovative visual qualities.

1941. Kane threatening the racketeer Jim Gettys (Ray Collins) *(above)* who will in fact ruin his opponent's political career—a sign of the décor and deep focus so important in *Citizen Kane.*

1941. Among many other things, *Kane* was a picture that grasped the confusion of politics and show business *(left)*. Welles was a close friend to FDR and it's clear that at this time of his life he had dreams of a political career—which, for Welles, meant nothing less than the big job.

1941. May 1, to be precise: the New York opening of *Citizen Kane (right)*, thanks to the courage of RKO in resisting offers from other film studios (to be paid off for junking the film because of its supposed lampooning of William Randolph Hearst). The reviews were outstanding, but in 1941 the audience found it a dark and difficult picture.

1949. Real politics hit the screen in Robert Rossen's version of Robert Penn Warren's novel *All the King's Men (left)*, based on the career of Louisiana senator Huey Long. It starred Broderick Crawford and Mercedes McCambridge.

1940s

1941. Best Picture for 1941 was not *Citizen Kane*, but John Ford's *How Green Was My Valley*. One of the features of the film was the re-creation of a small Welsh mining village (art direction by Richard Day and Nathan Juran). Maureen O'Hara and Walter Pidgeon in a scene from the film.

1942. Welles' second picture at RKO was *The Magnificent Ambersons,* about the decline of a wealthy midwestern family. Once the shooting was over, Welles left to attempt a documentary film in Brazil. In his absence, the studio shortened the film and gave it a happy ending. This is the ball scene, with Richard Bennett, Joseph Cotten, Dolores Costello, Don Dillaway, Agnes Moorehead, and Ray Collins.

1941. They said it was a version of *Snow White and the Seven Dwarfs*: burlesque dancer Barbara Stanwyck holes up with a team of learned lexicographers (look it up in the dictionary), led by Gary Cooper. It's *Ball of Fire*, directed by Howard Hawks.

1942. With America at war, Ernst Lubitsch's satire turned outrageous. In *To Be Or Not To Be*, a group of Polish actors have to play *Hamlet* for the Nazis. They are led by Carole Lombard and Jack Benny, seen in this still; Maude Eburne tends to Lombard's coif.

1943. Hemingway's Spanish Civil War story, *For Whom the Bell Tolls*, was shot in the California Sierra, and directed by Sam Wood. Gary Cooper was the American hero, and Ingrid Bergman played Maria. In this off-set photograph *(left)* they are reading over their lines.

1942. The sentimental romance of *Random Harvest (right)* was a major box-office hit, proving that Ronald Colman was still loved, and revealing Greer Garson as a big new star.

1942. Raoul Walsh's *Gentleman Jim* told the life story of heavyweight champion James J. Corbett, the Irish-American boxer who won the title in 1892—the first championship match fought with padded gloves. Errol Flynn played Jim *(left)*, seen here planting one on Sammy Stein's chin.

1941. One of the brightest
arrivals of the 1940s was director
Preston Sturges, previously an
inventor, a club-owner, and a
screenwriter, who put together a
string of delicious, warm satires
on Americana.

1942. In *Sullivan's Travels*, Joel
McCrea is an earnest film
director who resolves to find
harsh "reality," but who settles
for comedy—and a little
Veronica Lake.

1942. Another of the free-wheeling screwball pictures Sturges made was *The Palm Beach Story.* In this final scene in the film, Joel McCrea, Claudette Colbert, Rudy Vallee, Claudette Colbert, Joel McCrea, Mary Astor, and Sig Arno line up for a triple wedding (see the film to learn why). For five or six years, Sturges had the golden touch—but then it vanished. And never returned.

1940. As a screenwriter, Preston Sturges got a chance to direct on *The Great McGinty*—Paramount had one stipulation: they got the script for $1. Sturges's view of politics is infused with the same madness and exploitation. Brian Donlevy is the bum who gets to be mayor—he is with Muriel Angelus here.

1940. Alfred Hitchcock's first American film was *Rebecca*—which won producer David O. Selznick his second Best Picture Oscar in a row. In this still *(above)* the housekeeper, Mrs. Danvers (Judith Anderson), urges the second Mrs. de Winter (Joan Fontaine) to destroy herself.

1941. Got milk? More than that, Hitchcock put a small light in this glass of milk *(right)* so that it would glow, and Joan Fontaine was left wondering whether Cary Grant was trying to poison her—*Suspicion* anyone?

1940. A meeting of minds: Selznick and Hitchcock *(left)* on the *Rebecca* set. Selznick hired Hitch from England, argued with him, interfered in the projects, but launched his American career.

1945. Selznick fell in love with psychoanalysis, and the result was *Spellbound (left).* The film had Ingrid Bergman as one doctor rescuing another (played by Gregory Peck, one of the great romantic screen discoveries of the 1940s). There were superb, "Hitchcock" scenes in *Spellbound,* but it was agreed that Selznick was smothering his great director.

1945. Selznick commissioned designs for a dream sequence in *Spellbound* from the painter Salvador Dali. It was shot and then largely cut, but here we see Dali with Bergman *(right)* in her dream costume.

1943. Not a Selznick film, but one of Hitch's best: *Shadow of a Doubt (left)*, in which serial killer Uncle Charlie (Joseph Cotten) comes home to Santa Rosa, California, and begins to prey upon his niece Charlie (Teresa Wright). Also with Patricia Collinge.

1940s

1946. As Hitch made *Notorious* (*above*), Selznick was so busy on *Duel in the Sun* that Hitch felt free. It was his best American film yet, a dark love story mixed in with espionage, Cary Grant, and Ingrid Bergman.

1948, Hitchcock moved on, and in *Rope* (*right*) he experimented with the ten-minute take—very long elaborate shots. Here we see Farley Granger, James Stewart, and John Dall in a story based loosely on the famous 1924 Leopold–Loeb case, in which two wealthy college students murdered a neighbor's son.

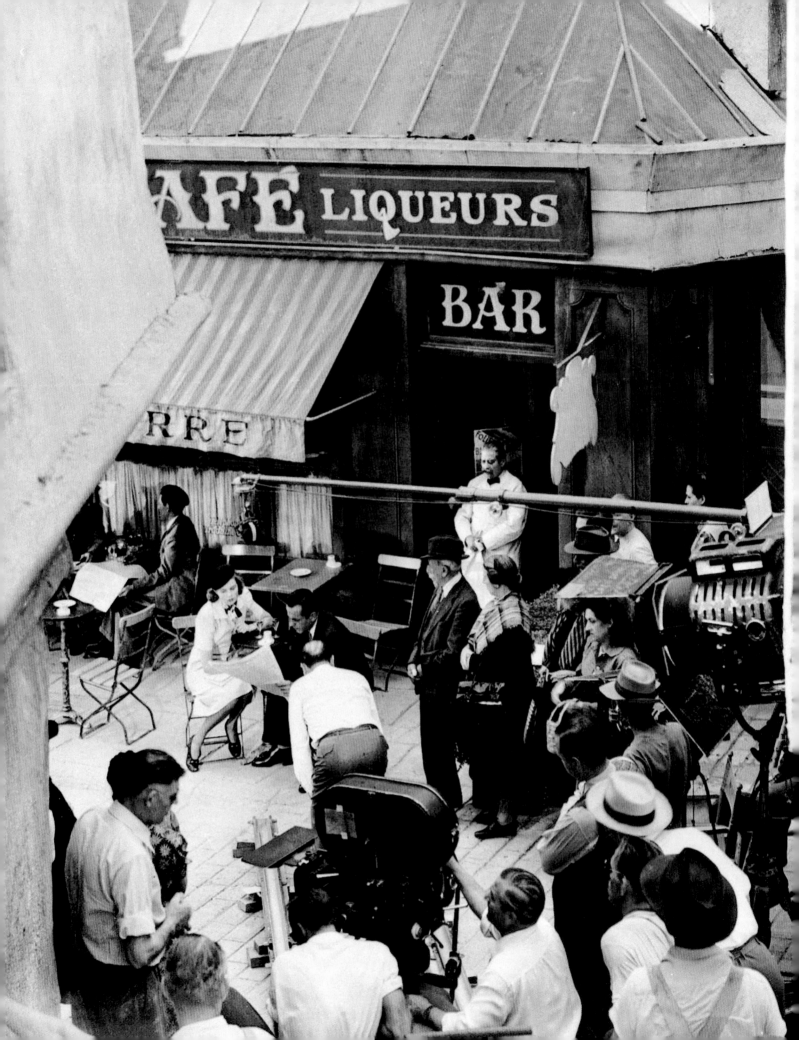

1942. The script was always changing. The casting was uncertain. It would turn out to be one of the greatest of "war" movies, yet the production never left California. Michael Curtiz was put in charge of it, and it would be called *Casablanca*. With Claude Rains, Paul Henreid, Humphrey Bogart, and Ingrid Bergman. Here is Curtiz rehearsing Bergman and Bogart *(left)* on the Parisian café set.

1942. Rick's café *(above)*. In *Casablanca*, Warners discovered the effectiveness of a café/cantina as a central setting. The piano player here is Dooley Wilson. *Casablanca* opened as Allied troops took the real city in North Africa. You can't beat publicity.

211

1942. Claude Rains is about to ask for the rounding up of the usual suspects *(left)*, while Paul Henreid, Bogart, and Bergman wait anxiously. It is a very romantic view of the war, perhaps, but one of those Hollywood moments we all know.

1942. Casablanca would win the Oscar for Best Picture and Best Director (Curtiz), and it has become the classic example of Hollywood's ability to convert every kind of creative uncertainty into stylish melodrama. It is also as good a display of moody black-and-white photography, rich supporting players *(above)*, and drop-dead lines as anyone could ask.

1944. *Gaslight* **entered** the English lexicon as a word meaning to "spook someone's imagination" with Patrick Hamilton's 1938 stage play, and then with George Cukor's film version *(left)*. The husband (Charles Boyer) wants his wife (Ingrid Bergman) to believe she is crazy. That would leave more time for the maid (Angela Lansbury) and what's up in the attic. Bergman won her first Oscar.

1944. It's another café, and this time Hoagy Carmichael is playing the piano for a new girl, Lauren Bacall. *To Have and Have Not* is based on Hemingway's novel, but we know it as one of Hollywood's most enchanted real-life love stories. Bogart meets Bacall. *To Have and Have Not (right)*, with sultry talk of cigarettes and whistling. Marcel Dalio enjoys the sport. And Howard Hawks is in charge— except that this time the seasoned womanizer didn't get the girl. Bogart did.

1949. One of George Cukor's best comedies, *Adam's Rib (left)*, starred lovers Tracy and Hepburn as a married couple who are also warring lawyers; newcomer Judy Holliday played the case in point.

1944. Barbara Stanwyck talking with Billy Wilder on the set of *Double Indemnity (left)*. Born in Sucha, Austria-Hungary in 1906, and trained as a reporter and screenwriter in Berlin, Wilder emigrated to America and worked for years as a writer, collaborating with his partner Charles Brackett on films such as *Ninotchka, Midnight,* and *Ball of Fire.*

1944. From the James M. Cain novel, with Raymond Chandler on the script, *Double Indemnity* was Wilder's breakthrough picture and the first unmistakable proof of his genius. The film was nominated for Best Picture and Best Director. It starred Barbara Stanwyck and Fred MacMurray *(right)* as snakes in love.

1945. Wilder followed up with *The Lost Weekend*, still one of the most frightening pictures about alcoholism ever attempted. Here are Ray Milland (Best Actor Oscar-winner) and Howard Da Silva *(left)*. The film also won Best Director, Best Picture, and Best Screenplay.

217

1940s

1943. Fritz Lang working in Hollywood on the set of *Scarlet Street (right)*. The arrogant German director was never too popular with crews and actors, but he stayed in America from 1936–56, and he made important contributions to the thriller and film noir.

1944. A séance scene from Lang's *The Ministry of Fear (left)*, adapted from the novel by Graham Greene. All his life, Lang liked to mix a sense of the occult with a dark view of human conspiracy.

1945. In *Scarlet Street* (adapted from Jean Renoir's French film, *La Chienne*, 1931), Lang cast Joan Bennett *(right)* as one of the great femmes fatales—"Lazy Legs," who seduces and nearly ruins Edward G. Robinson.

1941. In Lang's thriller *Man Hunt (above)*, Walter Pidgeon played a man who missed a chance of killing Hitler, and who was then caught up in chase and espionage. He's seen here with that expert child actor (and long-time Hollywood asset), Roddy McDowall.

1944. But Lang's masterpiece of the period is *The Woman in the Window (right)*, where Edward G. Robinson plays a happily married man alone in town, who is entranced by the portrait of a beautiful woman, turns, and sees the real thing next to him. Dream or reality? Again, it's Edward G. Robinson and Joan Bennett.

1944. Leo McCarey's *Going My Way* was a warm and sentimental film in which Barry Fitzgerald and Bing Crosby were a couple of Roman Catholic priests doing good in the world.

1944. *Going My Way* won Best Picture and Crosby and Fitzgerald got Oscars—the same year Ingrid Bergman won for *Gaslight*. Here they are together, just as McCarey set out to make *The Bells of St. Mary's* (with Ingrid as a nun) and Bing as the priest again.

1942. In the 1940s, the Road led to so many exotic places—Singapore, Zanzibar, Morocco, Utopia, Rio, and Bali—but Bob Hope and Bing Crosby rarely left the Paramount studio. The popularity of the pictures owed a lot to Dorothy Lamour, too. Here, in *Road to Morocco,* the boys face a fierce Arab (played by the young Anthony Quinn).

1948. Hope had another great hit in the spoof Western, *The Paleface*, where he played with Jane Russell.

1943. Religious themes continued in the 1940s with the story of a nineteenth-century French saint, *The Song of Bernadette (left)*, which won Jennifer Jones an Oscar. A few years earlier, Jones had been Phylis Isley, but then she was discovered by David O. Selznick. They became lovers. He changed her name and launched her new life.

1944. *Laura* was a smash hit *(right)*. It was Otto Preminger's effective debut and it concerned a murder—if you could be sure about the identity of the victim. It was witty, romantic, mysterious, and creepy and it had that great music (by David Raksin, who was not even nominated). It starred Gene Tierney, Dana Andrews (both seen here), and Clifton Webb.

1944. From the James M. Cain novel, *Mildred Pierce (left)* was a superb story of a mother who works all her life for a worthless daughter. The part was made for Joan Crawford, and Michael Curtiz guided her to the Oscar.

1940s

1943. Lena Horne is one of the greatest American entertainers least well served by the movies. But anyone interested should catch her singing the title song in *Stormy Weather (right)*, where she played with Bill "Bojangles" Robinson and Cab Calloway.

1943. The genius of the 1940s musical was director Vincente Minnelli who made *Cabin in the Sky*, an all-black picture, and one of the few decent film showcases for Lena Horne. Here we see Billy Rowe, Minnelli, and Horne talking to actor Melvyn Douglas *(left)*, who was visiting the set of *Cabin*.

1943. Eddie Anderson and Ethel Waters in a scene from *Cabin in the Sky (right)*, a groundbreaking musical, in which Waters sang "Happiness Is Just a Thing Called Joe."

1940. This is part of the scene from *Fantasia* where Mickey Mouse serves as "The Sorcerer's Apprentice" *(above)*. Enlisting Leopold Stokowski and the Philadelphia Orchestra, Disney attempted a heady blend of popular animation and high culture. It was a sign that Walt Disney had ambitions not just on film, but all of American culture.

1942. *Bambi* was an exquisite feature-length cartoon *(right)*, made against the grain of wartime, with amazing detail in the forest foliage. But the death of Bambi's mother remains one of the most devastating moments in American film.

1940. It's the story of a wooden puppet who longs to be a real boy. In *Pinocchio (left)*, Disney took the Carlo Collodi story, added a few elements, and delivered one of his classics—along with the song, "When You Wish Upon a Star."

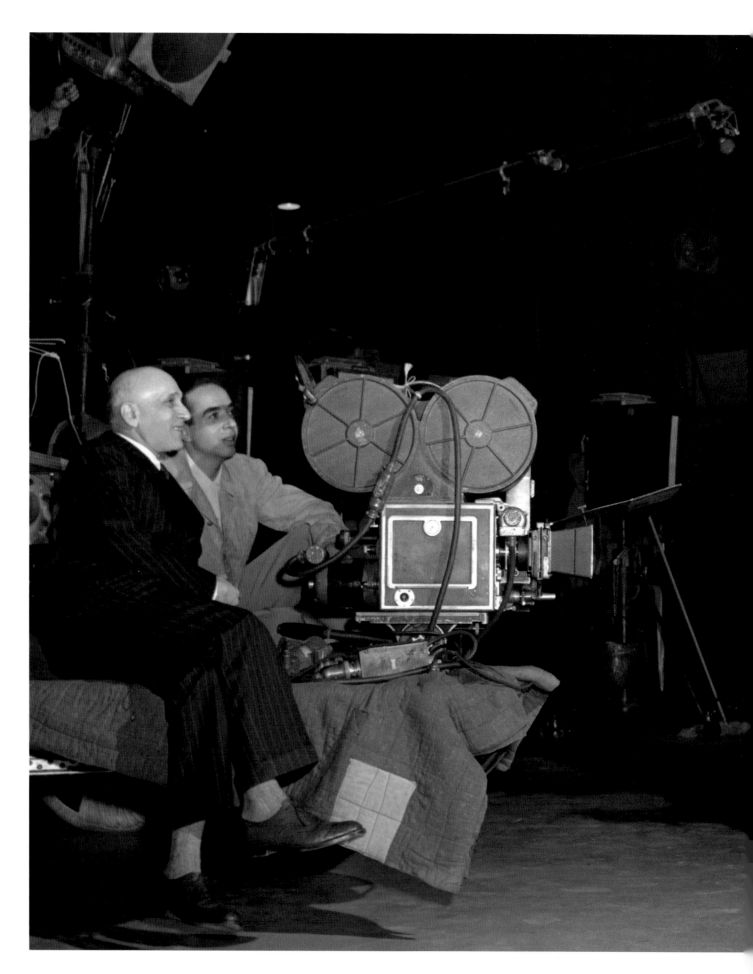

1944. Fred Astaire signed up with Metro in 1944, and did a duet with Gene Kelly in *The Ziegfeld Follies (left).* Here are the two great dancers of the age watched by Minnelli on set.

1942. Who could handle the song-and-dance, the comedy, the patriotism, and James Cagney playing George M. Cohan *(above)* in *Yankee Doodle Dandy*? Michael Curtiz could.

1945. *Anchors Aweigh* (*left*), directed by George Sidney, was a hit musical in the year of victories. It included Gene Kelly dancing with the cartoon mouse, Jerry, and Frank Sinatra singing "I Fall in Love Too Easily."

1949. Music by Leonard Bernstein, codirected by Gene Kelly and Stanley Donen: *On the Town (right)* was innovative in putting musical numbers in real places. *Left to right,* Frank Sinatra, Ann Miller, Jules Munshin, Vera-Ellen, Gene Kelly, and Betty Garrett.

1949. *It'a Great Feeling* was one of Warners' Doris Day musicals *(left).* Dennis Morgan and Jack Carson played the guys, and there was not the least hint of irony in the happy optimism. It would be years before Doris proved that she was more versatile.

1944. Where the enchantment of Americana meets the magic of the movies: *Meet Me in St. Louis*, directed by Vincente Minnelli, with Judy Garland and Margaret O'Brien doing "Under the Bamboo Tree." Garland and Minnelli would marry the following year.

1947. Garland and Gene Kelly in a scene from *The Pirate*, score by Cole Porter, direction by Minnelli. But the marriage to Minnelli was crumbling, and Judy was becoming harder to work with.

1947. On the set of *The Pirate*, Vincente Minnelli and Judy Garland, with their daughter, Liza. In fact, Judy was having love affairs (with Orson Welles and Joseph Mankiewicz) while Minnelli was attracted to men.

1948. *Easter Parade* was set to be Garland and Kelly, directed by Minnelli. But, as their marriage crumbled, so Garland said she couldn't work with Minnelli. Charles Walters stepped in. Then Gene Kelly broke an ankle and the way was clear for Astaire and Garland to do "A Couple of Swells".

1946. Lauren Bacall's first movie
was *To Have and Have Not,* in
1944. This poster from *The Big
Sleep (left)* shows how suddenly
Bacall—known as the "Look"—
had become a star.

1948. *Key Largo* was a John
Huston picture, made during the
same year as his award-winning
Treasure of the Sierra Madre. In
this off-set photo *(right)* Huston
(standing) rehearses Lionel
Barrymore, Bacall, and Bogart.

1948. *Key Largo* marooned
Bogart in a Florida hotel run by
Bacall and her father-in-law
(Barrymore). But the hotel was
overrun by a gang of thugs led
by Edward G. Robinson. This
scene *(left)* includes, *from left to
right,* William Haade, Barrymore,
Bogart, Harry Lewis, Thomas
Gomez, Dan Seymour, and
Bacall. Claire Trevor also
starred, as Robinson's abused
moll, winning her first and
only Oscar—for Best
Supporting Actress.

1940. Ronald Reagan and Jane Wyman met while filming *Brother Rat* (1938); two years later they were posing for this wedding photo. By 1948 she was winning the Best Actress Oscar in *Johnny Belinda* and he had just become president of the Screen Actors Guild—and they were close to divorce.

1940. The war itself was treated in unexpected ways. As early as 1940, Chaplin had done *The Great Dictator*, in which he impersonated a Hitler-like figure, and ended up delivering a warning sermon. Here's Charlie with his cameraman, Rollie Totheroh.

1942. *Mrs. Miniver,* directed by William Wyler, tried to show an English family coping with the war. It won several Oscars, including ones for Teresa Wright and Greer Garson (shown here), and it helped persuade American public opinion into seeing the necessity of war.

1946. Most potent of all was Wyler's *The Best Years of Our Lives*—about men home from the war. Here we see Hoagy Carmichael, Harold Russell (a soldier who had lost his hands), and Fredric March in the right foreground. Away in the left background—thanks to Gregg Toland's deep focus—Dana Andrews is making a phone call.

1944. It broke David Selznick's heart that he couldn't be involved in the war. So he made *Since You Went Away* as a tribute to the home front and the women left behind. Claudette Colbert is the mother and her daughters are played by Shirley Temple and Jennifer Jones. It was during this film that Jones's marriage to actor Robert Walker ended—and her affair with Selznick developed.

1949. After the war, combat films came into fashion. Few were better than Allan Dwan's *Sands of Iwo Jima* in which John Wayne (seen here with John Agar) was nominated for Best Actor as the tough Marine sergeant.

1949. In *I Was a Male War Bride,* the only way that Cary Grant (playing a French captain with no French accent) can get to the States with his wife (an American lieutenant) is . . . to become a woman. Only Howard Hawks could have been so daring. Ann Sheridan is the "wife."

1943. Another fabulous figure from the 1940s puts her best-loved parts in cement—Betty Grable at Grauman's Theatre. Betty's legs were not only loved—Fox had them insured for a million dollars by Lloyd's of London.

1940. One of the great screen openings: *The Letter (right)*, taken from the W. Somerset Maugham play, set in Malaya; married woman, Bette Davis, shoots her treacherous lover. Directed by William Wyler, Davis would never be better.

1946. Although ostensibly the villain, Rains gave another wonderful performance as Ingrid Bergman's husband in Alfred Hitchcock's post-war noir thriller *Notorious (left)*. Cary Grant also starred as the government agent who falls in love with Bergman but sends her into dangerous territory.

1944. One of the best romances of the era was *Mr. Skeffington (right)*, in which Bette Davis is the vain, spoiled wife of a Jewish businessman (Claude Rains)—who is long-suffering, rich, and a little dull.

1945. Our gallery of noir begins with *Detour*—more a C-movie than a B. Shot in six days (the legend goes), it is an astonishingly bleak portrait of meeting and murder. Directed by Edgar G. Ulmer, it stars Tom Neal and Ann Savage.

1946. *The Killers* **takes off** from the Hemingway short story of the same name and imagines the larger story. Directed by Robert Siodmak, it starred Ava Gardner and Burt Lancaster— and the amazing shadowy cinematography of Woody Bredell.

1946. At first it seemed that censorship would never allow a film version of James M. Cain's *The Postman Always Rings Twice.* But the problem was solved by a cleaned-up script, and the intense suggestiveness of Lana Turner and John Garfield.

1948. The conclusion of the movie *Criss Cross*, written by Daniel Fuchs and directed by Robert Siodmak again. It starred Lancaster, Yvonne De Carlo, and Dan Duryea in that classic triangle: good guy–femme fatale–bad guy.

1947. *Crossfire* **came from** a novel by Richard Brooks and was directed by Edward Dmytryk. The harshly contrasted black-and-white photography *(left)* covered a night world and the trail of anti-Semitism. It starred three Roberts: Ryan, Young, and Mitchum.

1947: *Crossfire* **was a great success**, but it was also a gathering of "suspicious" figures. This poster's tagline—"Hate is Like a Loaded Gun"—seems prophetic *(right)*. In time, director Edward Dmytryk, producer Adrian Scott, and screenwriter John Paxton would all be victims of the absurd and hypocritical Hollywood blacklist.

HATE IS LIKE A LOADED GUN!

DORE SCHARY *Presents*

ROBERT **YOUNG** · ROBERT **MITCHUM** · ROBERT **RYAN**

IN

"Crossfire"

WITH

GLORIA GRAHAME
PAUL KELLY · SAM LEVENE

Produced by ADRIAN SCOTT · *Directed by* EDWARD DMYTRYK
Screen Play by JOHN PAXTON

RKO RADIO

1948. Briefly married, Orson Welles and Rita Hayworth were already separated at the time of *The Lady from Shanghai*, and the love-hate shows. This is part of the final scene *(left),* shot at the Playland amusement park in San Francisco.

1948. Welles and Hayworth were one of those sensational but short-lived Hollywood couplings. It was the genius meets beauty for a moment. But she was afraid she bored him and weary of discovering that men couldn't see the insecure woman living behind the glamor of "Rita Hayworth." The couple play for the camera *(above)* in the dressing room during shooting *The Lady from Shanghai.*

1946. Here is Rita Hayworth as *Gilda* in the costume she wore for the "Put the Blame on Mame" number *(left)*. Ostensibly a femme fatale story, *Gilda* was also the provocative seed for future sexual politics.

1947. In *Out of the Past*, Robert Mitchum is trying to hide from his own past. But it catches up with him, and the flashbacks overlap with the present. Jacques Tourneur directed. Mitchum is seen here with Virginia Huston *(above)*, but the picture also starred Jane Greer and Kirk Douglas.

1947. The chilling new face (with the sneering voice) of Richard Widmark—as a psychotic killer, Tommy Udo, in Henry Hathaway's *Kiss of Death (right)*. He pushed an old woman in a wheelchair down a staircase, laughing all the time.

251

1945. Director John Ford had formed a documentary unit that covered real combat in the Pacific. Thus inspired, he returned to make *They Were Expendable*, about PT boats in the early days of the war. Here he is talking to one of the film's stars, Robert Montgomery *(left)*. The other star was John Wayne.

1946. The real Tombstone, Arizona was a rough, gold-rush place. But Ford celebrated the building of a new town fit for Republicans with *My Darling Clementine*. In this still we see Henry Fonda dancing on the floor of the new church with Cathy Downs *(right)*.

1948. In western history, there were no cavalry outposts in Monument Valley. But Ford couldn't resist the imagery of those buttes and lines of horsemen. This is a scene from *Fort Apache (left)*, which is a thinly disguised version of the story of Custer and the Sioux.

1946. By the mid-1940s, Leonard Slye (left) was king of the cowboys as far as kids were concerned. He called himself "Roy Rogers" now, and he usually played with his wife, Dale Evans, a sidekick, Gabby Hayes, and a horse called Trigger.

1946. The biggest Western of the era was *Duel in the Sun*, directed by King Vidor, but produced by David O. Selznick to show off the sexiness of Jennifer Jones (soon to be his second wife). This scene (right), with Gregory Peck, had to be censored in a production also known as "Lust in the Dust."

1948. The best Western was Howard Hawks's *Red River* (left), about a great cattle drive from Texas to Kansas, and the relationship between a father and his adopted son. It costarred Montgomery Clift, *right,* seen here with John Ireland.

1947. Another new comedy sensation was Danny Kaye, who played the lead in *The Secret Life of Walter Mitty*, as the daydreamer who gets tangled up in a real adventure. Kaye is seen here in a still from the film with Virginia Mayo.

1947. Clark Gable was a powerhouse in the 1930s (making nearly forty films). But in the 1940s, what with war service, age, and loss of confidence, he did only a dozen films. Here's his comeback after the war—*The Hucksters*, with Ava Gardner, Deborah Kerr (her first American picture), Gloria Holden, and Adolphe Menjou.

1947. Written by Moss Hart and directed by Elia Kazan, *Gentleman's Agreement* took on anti-Semitism, and starred Dorothy McGuire and Gregory Peck. It won Best Picture, Best Director, and Best Supporting Actress (Celeste Holm).

1948. Olivia de Havilland came into her own in the mid-1940s. She won one Oscar in the Mitchell Leisen romance, *To Each His Own*. Then she won again in 1949 in *The Heiress*, adapted from Henry James. But her most controversial film was *The Snake Pit* (seen here), directed by Anatole Litvak, which tried to show the quality of life in an American asylum.

1948. Max Ophüls was one more European director who came to America as a refugee (he was from Germany). His most perfect American film was *Letter from an Unknown Woman*, starring Louis Jourdan and Joan Fontaine.

1949. Ophüls made *Caught*— about a model and a tycoon (Barbara Bel Geddes and Robert Ryan)—and encouraged Ryan to base the role on Howard Hughes. Ophüls (seated in center) watches the action on set with James Mason (on far left), who also starred, and Bel Geddes (on far right).

1949. Technically and spiritually it was a British film, shot in London and Vienna. Still, Carol Reed's *The Third Man* needed Selznick's money and two American stars— Joseph Cotten and Orson Welles. It also indicated how necessary coproduction was going to be in the new age.

1949. Still going strong, and making it as far as the Top of the World, it's James Cagney as gangster Cody Jarrett in Raoul Walsh's *White Heat*.

1949. King Vidor turned Ayn Rand's novel *The Fountainhead* into a dazzling and controversial film. Gary Cooper played the architect Howard Roark, and Patricia Neal was the woman who loves and hates him *(left)*.

1948. A connoisseur of Mexico, John Huston loved B. Traven's story of gold and the fools it makes of men. *The Treasure of the Sierra Madre (above)* starred Bogart with Huston's own father, Walter. It is still one of the best of adventure films and it lost Best Picture only to Olivier's Hamlet. But Walter Huston won for supporting actor and John Huston for director and screenplay.

1943. Jane Russell *(right)* was famous for the many delays in *The Outlaw* (begun in 1941 by Howard Hawks and not released until 1943 as a Howard Hughes film). The movie made a great deal of Russell's breasts (though God and parentage had been there first). Some posters said there were two big reasons for seeing the picture.

1946. Though not an immediate hit, Frank Capra's *It's a Wonderful Life (left)* was a telling portrait of anxieties in the new America. It would become one of the most beloved of pictures, and a Christmas regular. The family group here includes Thomas Mitchell, Donna Reed, James Stewart, and on the far right, Beulah Bondi.

1944. Elizabeth Taylor and Mickey Rooney in a scene from *National Velvet (above)*. Taylor grew up in the 1940s, in Hollywood, and no child actress had a bigger future waiting.

1950s

1950s

High Fever in the Atomic Age

One could claim, as President Eisenhower did, that America in the 1950s was prosperous and happy, with a car, a refrigerator, 2.5 children, and a television in every home. But there was tension in the air and in the suburban utopia: the Cold War and fears of the bomb; the paranoia of Joe McCarthy on television; the Montgomery bus boycott; the feeling that sex was there and kids wanted it; the throb of rock and roll; the way Marilyn Monroe seemed ready to burst out of her clothes; James Dean on the brink of violence.

The movies had their own threat: it was that TV set, which was imprisoning Americans in their perfect living rooms. So movies tried to be different with 3–D, CinemaScope, and even Smell-o-Vision. There were pictures, like *Sunset Boulevard* and *The Bad and the Beautiful*, that suggested Hollywood was a terrible place and a bad influence. Or was it that the movies needed to grow up?

Yet the screen was full of attractive new players— Elizabeth Taylor, William Holden, Montgomery Clift, Rock Hudson, Audrey Hepburn, Grace Kelly . . . Dean, Elvis, and Marilyn. So the 1950s were a time of films Ike would not have liked—*A Streetcar Named Desire, Rebel Without a Cause, On the Waterfront, 12 Angry Men, Vertigo, Some Like It Hot*—as well as others that he could point to and say, look, everything's okay: musicals like *An American in Paris* and *Singin' in the Rain*; classic westerns, from *High Noon* to *Shane; The Greatest Show on Earth; Around the World in 80 Days; Gigi; Ben-Hur*; and all that sweet Doris Day.

1950. Get out the car, and let's drive to Paramount *(right)*. Norma Desmond (Gloria Swanson) is making a comeback. Joe Gillis (William Holden) is her tame writer. And Max Von Mayerling (Erich von Stroheim) is ex-director, ex-husband, and chauffeur. *Sunset Boulevard*, Billy Wilder's acid reappraisal of Hollywood. And all Paramount really wants is to hire the car!

1950. Sunset Boulevard was not the easiest picture to cast, for actors were fearful of the scathing tone. So Mary Pickford and Montgomery Clift declined, and we now regard Gloria Swanson and William Holden as the inevitable and essential figures. In this on-set photo *(left)* Wilder directs Swanson as Holden looks on.

1950. The finale of *Sunset Boulevard (right)*. A murderess now, Norma goes off with the police, playing it all as her big scene. "I'm ready for my close up."

1950. In Nicholas Ray's *In a Lonely Place*, Humphrey Bogart plays a violent, disillusioned screenwriter who falls in love with Gloria Grahame. But the title refers to the difficulty of doing good work and living in Hollywood.

1950. The bumpy night—the party in *All About Eve*, Joseph L. Mankiewicz's witty satire on the romance of theater. *From left to right,* Anne Baxter as the opportunist Eve, Bette Davis as grand star Margo Channing, Marilyn Monroe as Miss Caswell, and George Sanders as critic Addison De Witt.

1950. Joe Mankiewicz
also directed one of the most stinging attacks on racism, *No Way Out,* in which Richard Widmark played the bigot. The same movie introduced two newcomers—Sidney Poitier and Ruby Dee *(left).*

1952. In Vincente Minnelli's
The Bad and the Beautiful, the title alludes to the gods and goddesses of picture-making. Here we see Kirk Douglas as a Selznick-like producer, and Lana Turner as a Turnesque star.

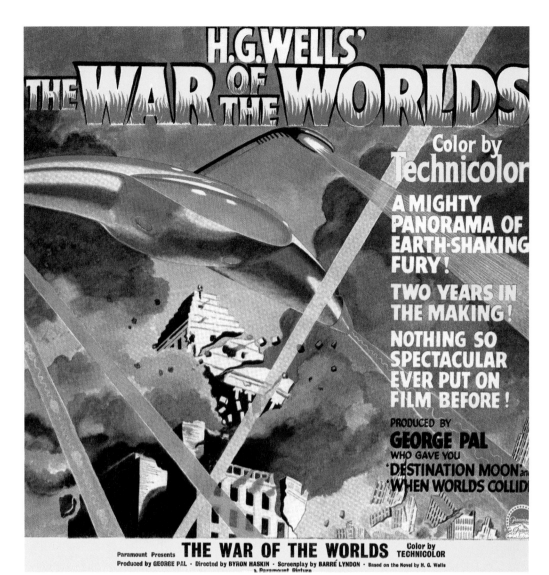

1953. The War of the Worlds had a great history—it had been the basis for the 1938 radio show in which Orson Welles scared the nation. George Pal's 1953 version *(left)* was famous for its special effects. Pal, Hungarian by birth, and a sci-fi enthusiast, won the special effects Oscar five times—twice as a director (most famously for *The Time Machine,* 1960) and three times as a producer.

1951. *The Day the Earth Stood Still* has a deservedly high reputation. It's about aliens who visit Earth to warn against nuclear weapons. Here we see Patricia Neal and Michael Rennie *(left)* with a robot. It was directed by the enormously versatile Robert Wise, who would excel in every known genre.

1954. In *Them!*, nuclear fallout has given ants an evolutionary boost. It is one of the most suspenseful science-fiction films ever produced, directed by Gordon Douglas. In this still *(right)* Joan Weldon is terrorized by a hungry ant.

1954. If your picture is Amazing! Startling! Shocking! admit it on the poster *(left)*. Even if it isn't, say so. *Creature from the Black Lagoon* may be the most famous creature film because when the Marilyn Monroe character in *The Seven Year Itch* saw it, she sympathized with the Creature.

1954. Every Creature wants to look his or her best, and *Creature from the Black Lagoon (left)* is a high point in rubber-suit transformations. The film was directed by Jack Arnold, who also did *It Came from Outer Space* and *The Incredible Shrinking Man.*

1956. The masterpiece of the genre is Don Siegel's *Invasion of the Body Snatchers,* in which people start turning into dehumanized pod-people. Here we see Siegel directing Dana Wynter and Kevin McCarthy *(right)* when they are the last warm couple left.

1951. *An American in Paris*— about an American painter living in Paris—seemed like the artistic highpoint of the musical. It included a dream sequence in which Gene Kelly and Leslie Caron danced in the worlds of great painters—here it is the mood of Henri Rousseau *(right).*

1952. The very next year, Kelly and codirector Stanley Donen topped it all with a musical about the moment when sound came to Hollywood—*Singin' in the Rain.* Gene Kelly and Cyd Charisse dance the *Broadway Ballet (left).*

1952. Kelly's iconic moment from the great *Singin' in the Rain (right).*

1953. Doris Day had entered the movies in the late 1940s, but she became a dominant star in the 1950s. Here she is in one of her biggest hits, *Calamity Jane*, the film where she sang "Secret Love."

1953. Crossover time. Betty Grable had been a star since the late 1930s, and the essential leggy pinup of the war years. But in *How to Marry a Millionaire*, she starred with her nemesis—Marilyn Monroe, the new sex goddess. The film also included Lauren Bacall.

1954. In one film together, *Young at Heart*, Doris Day and Frank Sinatra had tremendous chemistry. But no one thought to try again.

1954. *Seven Brides for Seven Brothers* was another of the great musicals, full of athletic dance numbers—Stanley Donen directed and Michael Kidd did the choreography. And Howard Keel (seen in the right foreground) and Jane Powell were the leads.

1954. History is made. *Carmen Jones* was the Georges Bizet opera, reset in the American South, with lyrics by Oscar Hammerstein. Dorothy Dandridge (*left,* in a promotional portrait for the film) was Carmen (though Marilyn Horne sang for her). But under Otto Preminger's direction, she became the first black nomination for a lead-acting Oscar.

1954. Judy Garland made her comeback in a musical version of *A Star is Born (right),* with James Mason playing her husband. George Cukor directed, and there were great scenes, but the film was too long (three hours) for public taste.

1955. There was also a run of stage musicals transported to the screen—like *Oklahoma!,* where Gordon MacRae and Shirley Jones were in "The Surrey with the Fringe on Top" *(left).*

281

1956. "Shall we dance?" Anna teaches the King of Siam in *The King and I*, directed by Walter Lang and starring Yul Brynner and Deborah Kerr.

1956. Another Rodgers and Hammerstein hit show was *Carousel*, directed by Henry King. Gordon MacRae and Shirley Jones, the romantic leads in *Oklahoma!*, star again as lovers (they are joined here by Barbara Ruick, *far right*). Jones was that rarity—an actress who could also sing her own songs.

1956. Nothing was as enchanting as a small musical, made for the movies: *Funny Face*, directed by Stanley Donen, and pairing Fred Astaire with Audrey Hepburn. Here is one of the great faces of the 1950s in a candid moment between scenes.

1957. Not far short of sixty, Astaire danced with Cyd Charisse in Rouben Mamoulian's *Silk Stockings*—a musical remake of *Ninotchka*, with songs by Cole Porter.

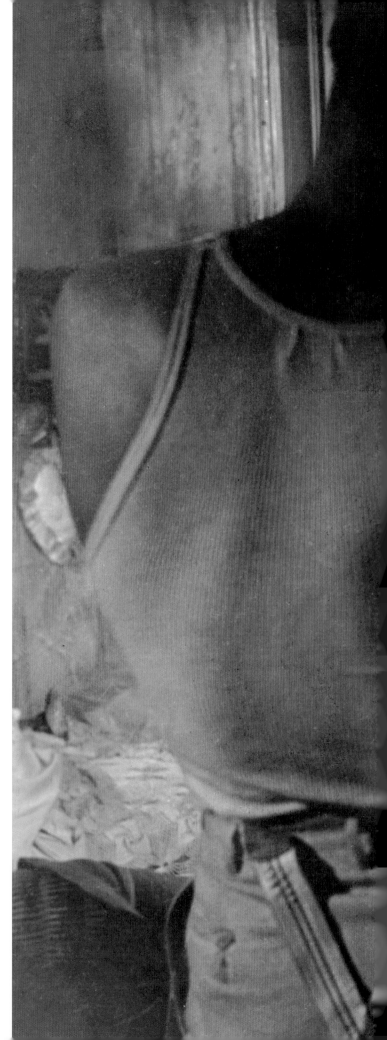

1950. Marlon Brando came from Omaha, Nebraska, and he had been thrown out of military school. He could seem tough and poetic at the same time, and had been chosen personally by Tennessee Williams to play Stanley in *A Streetcar Named Desire* (he poses for a wardrobe test, *above*). To this day, Brando stands as a model for actors; and as a mystery man who turned his back on movies.

1951. Though the movie had to be tamed by the censors, Elia Kazan's *A Streetcar Named Desire* was an important event— for it reproduced the stunning stage performance of Marlon Brando, seen here with Vivien Leigh *(right)*, who won her second Oscar as the Southern belle Blanche DuBois.

1953. "What are you rebelling against?" someone asks Brando's character in *The Wild One*. "What have you got?" he answers. The film has dated, but it helped establish Brando as the leather-jacketed poet-outsider of the age *(left)*.

1954. The hot director and the hot actor *(right)*. Elia Kazan was a triumph as a stage director in the late 1940s. In 1952 he testified to the House Un American Activities Committee and his film career took off. *On the Waterfront*, starring Brando, won lots of Oscars, and it also endorsed informing.

1954. Eva Marie Saint and Brando in a scene from *On the Waterfront (left)*. He won Best Actor and she took Best Supporting Actress.

1953. In Billy Wilder's *Stalag 17* *(right),* William Holden, *center,* played a cynical prisoner of war who resists team spirit. It turns out that he's a good guy after all, as well as a survivor. Seen here with a bearded Robert Strauss, Holden took the Oscar.

1953. They said that James Jones's *From Here to Eternity* couldn't be filmed. Writer Daniel Taradash and director Fred Zinnemann proved them wrong and the film was famous for this beach love scene with Burt Lancaster and Deborah Kerr *(left).*

1951. Darkness was spreading. In *Ace in the Hole* (also by Billy Wilder), Kirk Douglas played a newspaperman who tries to control a mining accident to make himself famous *(right).* No actor was happier playing heels than Douglas.

1950s

1953. Fritz Lang was still working in the 1950s, and he produced one of his very best pictures in *The Big Heat*. Glenn Ford was the star. But the relationship between Lee Marvin as the vicious gangster and Gloria Grahame as his moll drew attention—watch out for that glass coffee pot at bottom right.

1957. Maybe the most startling and unsentimental film of the era was *Sweet Smell of Success*, written by Ernest Lehman and Clifford Odets and directed by Alexander Mackendrick. Burt Lancaster plays the cruel newspaper columnist J. J. Hunsecker (based loosely on Walter Winchell) and Tony Curtis is the obsequious press agent Sidney Falco.

1954. *Suddenly* was a small film, about a man who plans to shoot the president. But Frank Sinatra was the man. He had won an Oscar in *From Here to Eternity*, but now it was clear—he could act, and he had a nasty streak. Sinatra is here with Nancy Gates.

1955. The next year, Sinatra was superb as a drug addict in *The Man with the Golden Arm*. He is seen here, rehearsing, with director Otto Preminger leaning over his shoulder.

1951. She had been a child star and a teenage favorite, but now a major career was dawning—that of Elizabeth Taylor. Only eighteen, she did the ravishing love scenes with Montgomery Clift in George Stevens's *A Place in the Sun (right)*.

1956. Five years later, for Stevens again, Taylor played the Eastern girl who becomes a Texas matriarch in *Giant*. In one of the film's best scenes *(left)* she meets Jett Rink (James Dean). In fact, Dean's career was nearly over, but what few appreciated was that Liz was his junior.

1958. She was so beautiful in an age when desire and censorship were pulling in opposite directions. Here she is, taking a nap, while crewmen work on a set for *Suddenly Last Summer (right)*. Taylor had lived so many lives already—but the future would be so much more turbulent.

1955. The essential new face of the 1950s, enormously romanticized by the way he was gone almost before he had registered: James Dean (1931–55). With one pained glance, the basis of movies shifted toward youth. This close-up still is from *East of Eden (left)*.

1955. *East of Eden* was an adaptation of the John Steinbeck novel, directed by Elia Kazan. It was set in the era of World War I and concentrated on the lives and problems of the kids. Here we see Dean with Julie Harris *(right)*.

1955. *Rebel Without a Cause* was the one Dean film set in modern-day America. It was a portrait of high school in Los Angeles, directed by Nicholas Ray. *From left to right,* Sal Mineo, Dean, and Corey Allen, just before the "Chicken Run."

1951. It's generally agreed that the 1950s were the supreme age of Alfred Hitchcock. After a small slump, he came back with *Strangers on a Train (right)*, adapted from the Patricia Highsmith novel. Farley Granger, *left*, and Robert Walker, *right*, discuss the possibility of swapping murders.

PARAMOUNT presents

JAMES STEWART DORIS DAY

ALFRED HITCHCOCK'S

THE MAN WHO KNEW TOO MUCH

COLOR BY TECHNICOLOR

DIRECTED BY ALFRED HITCHCOCK · SCREENPLAY BY JOHN MICHAEL HAYES · BASED ON A STORY BY CHARLES BENNETT AND D. B. WYNDHAM-LEWIS

1956. Hitchcock had done *The Man Who Knew Too Much* in England in the 1930s, in black and white. The remake, in color *(left)*, was a vehicle for James Stewart and Doris Day, who managed to slip a hit song, "Whatever Will Be," into the suspense story.

1954. The perfect Hitchcock film, with the perfect Hitchcock heroine? James Stewart is a photographer with a broken leg. With nothing to do, he spies on his neighbors, and one night, across the courtyard, he sees . . . ? Grace Kelly and James Stewart at a key moment in *Rear Window (right)*.

1955. Another career that meant all the more for being cut off early was that of Grace Kelly. Of course, she went from being the princess of Hollywood to taking up the real job in Monaco. It was during the filming of Hitchcock's *To Catch a Thief* that Kelly met Prince Rainier of Monaco, who actually censored the love scenes from the film, with Cary Grant *(right)*.

1955. Hitchcock loved cool blondes, and there is no doubt but that the eroticism of his films began in his own daydreams. Here he is speaking words of wisdom and woo to Grace Kelly on the set of *To Catch a Thief (left)*—even when she was a princess, he tried to get her to come back to make more films.

1956. Grace Kelly made only eleven pictures, and though she won an Oscar (for *The Country Girl*) it wasn't that she was so good an actress. It was more that people adored her—those close and those far away. And she had what was called a fairy-story arc— the film star who becomes royal. The truth was less pretty maybe, but Kelly is an icon. This portrait was for *High Society (right)*, her last Hollywood film, and a musical remake of *The Philadelphia Story*.

1958. Over the years, *Vertigo* has come to be recognized as one of Hitchcock's masterpieces. It seems to be a story about an ex-detective (James Stewart) following a woman with a death wish (Kim Novak). But the plot thickens—and why is a man with vertigo living in San Francisco?

1958. Had she stayed around, it might have been Grace Kelly in *Vertigo*. Instead, Hitchcock used another 1950s blonde, Novak. Here she is, talking to the master.

1959. As if needing a lighter mood, Hitch stepped back and did a kind of screwball mystery story—*North by Northwest*, in which Eva Marie Saint and Cary Grant end up hanging on to the Mt. Rushmore monument for dear life.

1959. The classic Hitchcock set-piece. In the middle of flat, prairie Americana, why is that plane dusting crops where no crops grow? Cary Grant in *North by Northwest* (written by Ernest Lehman).

1950s

1954. Another essential star in the uneasy 1950s was Rock Hudson. Groomed at Universal, he became a he-man, a ladies' man, a gentle Rock. Here he is with Jane Wyman in Douglas Sirk's *Magnificent Obsession (right)*.

1959. Rock cuddles with Doris Day in *Pillow Talk (left)*, which was an attempt at sophisticated sexual comedy that only suggested the sensual explosion to come in the 1960s.

1957. Hudson was the lead in *Giant* before playing Hemingway's war hero (with Jennifer Jones) in *A Farewell to Arms (right)*, which was also the swansong of David O. Selznick.

1952. It was an age of great Westerns, and *High Noon* had undertones that made it all the more intriguing. The sheriff (Gary Cooper) wants the town's support in a crisis—but everyone has reasons for opting out. The suspense masterpiece worked as an allegory on McCarthyism, and won Cooper the Best Actor Oscar.

1953. Just as profound was *Shane*, in which Alan Ladd is the wandering gunfighter who chooses to help the farmers in their fight against ranchers. George Stevens directed. Ladd is seen here with Brandon de Wilde.

1954. Even Native American stories were told with more honesty and sympathy in the 1950s. In Robert Aldrich's *Apache*, Burt Lancaster played the rebel chief who resists white authority.

1955. A modern-day Western: in *Bad Day at Black Rock* (directed by John Sturges) Spencer Tracy comes to a Nevada town to honor a Japanese-American who fought in the war. But he finds a pit of corruption and the threats of Ernest Borgnine, one of the best heavies of the era.

1956. Wyatt Earp's story has been told over and over again—with varying degrees of accuracy. *Gunfight at the O.K. Corral,* directed by John Sturges, was as clear-cut as Cold War antagonisms. It had Burt Lancaster as Wyatt and Kirk Douglas as Doc Holliday.

1955. Anthony Mann (with his regular star, James Stewart) made a string of fine Westerns: *Winchester 73, Bend of the River, The Far Country, The Naked Spur* and, here, *The Man from Laramie.* Stewart proves his stalwartness time and again in these films; in this scene, he is roped and dragged through a campfire, but worse was still to come.

1956. The wanderer walks away from civilization and back into the desert—the last image of John Ford's *The Searchers*, with John Wayne.

1959. Howard Hawks came back to the Western too, and made a kind of situation comedy out of it. Sheriff John Wayne has real villains to handle in *Rio Bravo*, but it's the talk, the thinking, and the sexual candor of Angie Dickinson that throws him most.

1950s

1952. The 1950s was the age in which television took over the world. In response, the movies tried to be bigger, better, something you had never seen before. Cecil B. DeMille coined the title of this attitude *The Greatest Show on Earth*, *(previous pages)* a circus story that won Best Picture. This group includes James Stewart (the clown), Charlton Heston, (on stretcher) and Betty Hutton (in striped robe).

1953. Twentieth Century Fox developed a new wide-screen system, CinemaScope, which soon had stereophonic sound added to it. The first Scope film was the religious epic *The Robe (right)*, starring Richard Burton and Jean Simmons.

1956. The biggest epic of the age was DeMille's remake of his 1923 film—*The Ten Commandments*. With sound, the characters became more intriguing and even neurotic—as demonstrated by the Pharaoh of Yul Brynner, seen here with Anne Baxter as Queen Nefritiri *(left)*.

1956. But *The Ten Commandments* relied on its Moses, and in Charlton Heston the canny DeMille identified the hero of the age—a man of action and conscience. The world was ready to be cynical, but DeMille succeeded again, and nowhere as fully as in the Golden Calf scene *(right)*, as God strikes down the sinners.

1950s

1956. Showman Mike Todd had tried to put Jules Verne's *Around the World in 80 Days* on stage in the 1940s (with Orson Welles directing). He persevered, and in 1956 the movie won Best Picture. It starred David Niven and newcomer Shirley MacLaine *(right)*.

1959. Director George Stevens had been deeply affected by his wartime experience (as a serviceman, he photographed the liberation of Dachau). This could be felt in *The Diary of Anne Frank*, though newcomer Millie Perkins *(left)*, from Passaic, New Jersey, acted oddly like an American teenager as the Dutch girl.

1957. Another epic reexamined the war in Burma and the role of prisoners of war. *The Bridge on the River Kwai* was directed by David Lean, and Alec Guinness played a very British officer *(right)*. But it was a coproduction, with a lot of American money (and William Holden) to balance the stiff upper lip.

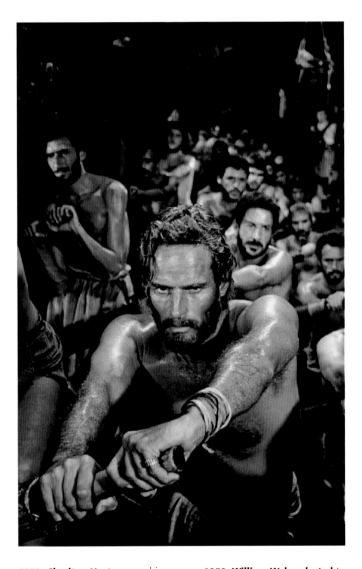

1959. Charlton Heston won his Oscar for *Ben-Hur (*the film won a total of 11 Oscars--only James Cameron's *Titanic* has won as many). Heston plays the Jewish prince Judah Ben-Hur, who was sold into slavery by a Roman friend (he is seen, *above,* in the galleys) but triumphs in the end. Known now as much for his political stance as his acting, Heston is that rare thing—a formerly great star who is now happy to play small roles. In short, a professional.

1959. William Wyler elected to remake the 1925 silent film *Ben-Hur*. It took $15 million, six years of shooting, and thousands of extras, and was the most expensive film ever made at the time. The chariot race (with Charlton Heston and Stephen Boyd, *right*), was better than ever, but critics and audiences alike admired the adult treatment of the story.

1953. William Wyler did a lot in the 1950s, ranging from *Ben-Hur* to the delightful comedy *Roman Holiday*, which was the effective introduction of Audrey Hepburn to the world. Hepburn won audiences over with her portrayal of a princess playing hooky on holiday, and she also won the Oscar. Gregory Peck played the reporter pretending to be a tour guide.

1954. Billy Wilder's *Sabrina* put Audrey Hepburn between William Holden and Humphrey Bogart (here she shares the front seat with Holden). It was one among several examples of young women on screen (like *Rear Window, In a Lonely Place,* and *Rio Bravo*) that were seemingly happy with much older men.

1950. When catching up on the great entertainments of the era, don't forget George Cukor's version of Garson Kanin's play *Born Yesterday,* with Judy Holliday, Broderick Crawford, and William Holden. Holliday won the Oscar—beating out Bette Davis in *All About Eve* and Gloria Swanson in *Sunset Boulevard.*

1954. Joseph Levitch meets Dino Crocetti. The comedy sensation of the 1950s, Dean Martin and Jerry Lewis had teamed up in the late 1940s, playing nightclubs. They made sixteen films together in ten years, after which Dean acted and Jerry concentrated on directing and his annual telethon.

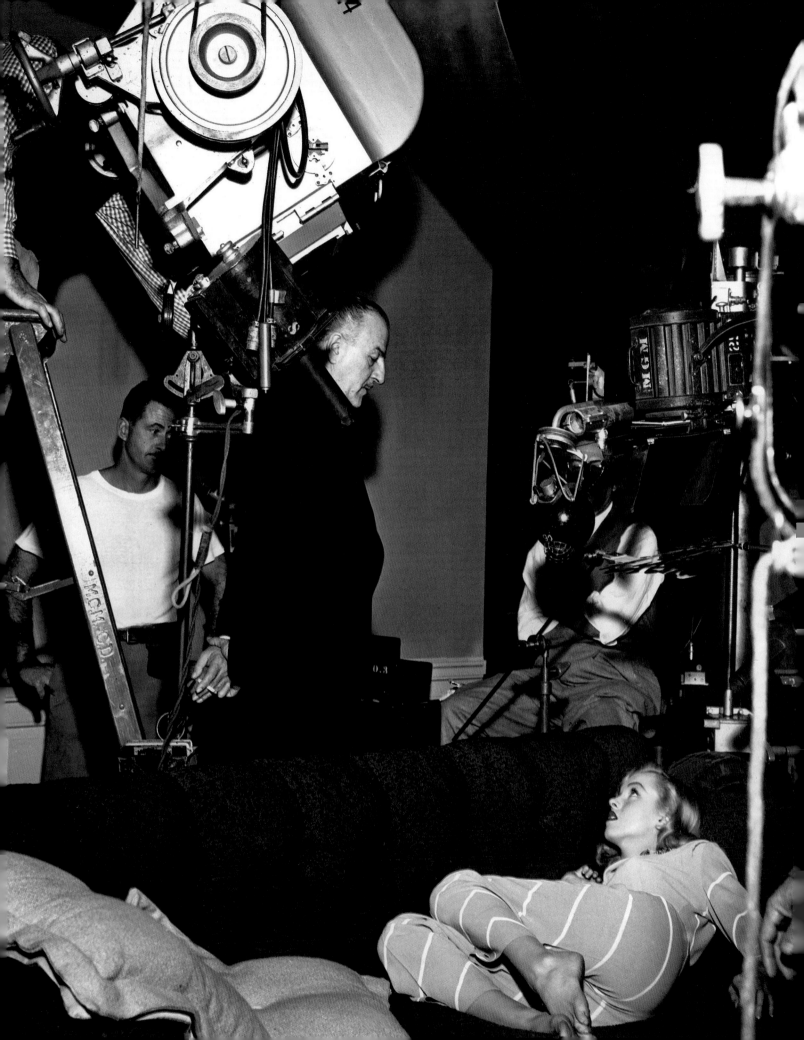

1950. Marilyn Monroe was creeping into good films in small parts—not just *All About Eve*, but in dark thrillers like John Huston's *The Asphalt Jungle*, where she plays the mistress to Louis Calhern. Calhern and Monroe film a scene in this on-set photo *(left)*.

1953. The thing no one doubted about Marilyn was how great she looked in stills. This is a portrait for Howard Hawks's *Gentlemen Prefer Blondes (above)*.

319

1956. Some say that Marilyn was never more touching than in *Bus Stop*, with the fond attention of Don Murray *(left)*. Joshua Logan directed.

1955. In Billy Wilder's *The Seven Year Itch*, Marilyn's character liked to feel the rush of subway air on a warm night *(left)*. Tom Ewell is watching. It was having to watch this scene filmed that broke up her marriage to Joe DiMaggio.

1959. "I'm a girl, I'm a girl!" A moment from one of the most sublime (and naughty) American comedies—it's Marilyn with husband Arthur Miller and Jack Lemmon on the set of Billy Wilder's *Some Like it Hot (right)*. Tony Curtis (who played Monroe's girlfriend and boyfriend) was still in makeup.

1955. Kirk Douglas takes his son to visit the studio *(right)*. Is this the day Michael Douglas started to wonder what he might become?

1951. Detective Story (directed by William Wyler from the play by Sidney Kingsley) took advantage of Kirk Douglas's self-torturing capacity for pain. It would also prove a model for all those TV shows to come set in police precinct stations. In this scene he gives the treatment to burglar Joseph Wiseman *(left)*.

1956. Douglas continued to grow more important as the 1950s went on. He showed what an actor he could be playing Vincent Van Gogh in Vincente Minnelli's *Lust for Life (right)*.

1951. John Huston took everyone to Africa, knowing the reality would transform the odd romance of *The African Queen*—with Bogart as the skipper and Katharine Hepburn as his passenger.

1954. Herman Wouk's best-selling novel, *The Caine Mutiny*, became a movie directed by Edward Dmytryk. Bogart did one of his best acting jobs as the jittery Captain Queeg, and Van Johnson played the leader of the mutiny.

1952. John Ford's romantic feelings for Ireland found fruition in several films, including *The Quiet Man*, with John Wayne and Maureen O'Hara.

1953. John Ford took the old Gable classic, *Red Dust* (set in Indochina), shifted it to Africa and called it *Mogambo*. Mary Astor and Jean Harlow became Grace Kelly and Ava Gardner, but Gable stayed Gable.

1950s

1955. *Marty* had been a TV play by Paddy Chayefsky (with Rod Steiger in the lead). When they did the movie, Ernest Borgnine was cast. At the Oscars, it won Best Picture, Best Director, and there was another award for Borgnine.

1955. Actor Charles Laughton longed to direct a film. He chose the Davis Grubb novel, *The Night of the Hunter*, and cast Robert Mitchum as the villain. In its day, the film flopped completely, but now it is hailed as an American masterpiece. Mitchum threatens Sally Jane Bruce and Billy Chapin in this still.

1956. A young New Yorker named Stanley Kubrick was beginning his career and he drew attention with a tight little horse-track robbery film, *The Killing. From left to right,* the crew schemes around the table: Jay C. Flippen, Joe Sawyer, Ted de Corsia, Elisha Cook Jr., and Sterling Hayden.

1955. From a William Inge play, *Picnic* was helped by William Holden and Susan Strasberg (seen here) as well as Kim Novak. But what everyone remembers is George Duning's score.

1950s

1958. No one quite realized it at the time, but Vincente Minnelli's *Gigi* was the end of the MGM musical. Based on the 1945 novel by Colette, it starred, *from left to right,* Louis Jourdan, Leslie Caron, and Hollywood's perfect Frenchman, Maurice Chevalier.

1955. Among animated films, Disney's romantic *Lady and the Tramp (left)* was a standout. It was the first feature-length cartoon to use wide-screen CinemaScope.

1957. It wasn't just his movies, of course. Elvis Presley (coming right after James Dean) was the new kid. The future King does the grind in *Jailhouse Rock (right)*.

1958. A read-through of *The Long, Hot Summer (left)*, with director Ritt, Newman, Woodward, Anthony Franciosa, producer Jerry Wald, Maguerite Lamkin, Lee Remick, and Orson Welles, who gave one of his hammiest performances as the landowner.

1958. Paul Newman and Joanne Woodward were Hollywood's new ideal couple. But it was a large error to think that they could play William Faulkner the way Faulkner intended. *The Long, Hot Summer (left)*, directed by Martin Ritt, still stands as proof of Hollywood's uncertain grasp of the South, and its nervousness with Faulkner's material.

1957. Joanne Woodward (being congratulated by Newman, *right*), won the Oscar for her performance in *The Three Faces of Eve.* They were married the next year. In the future, Newman would direct his wife in several films.

1957. The mark of TV again: a single-set drama, the jury room filled with *12 Angry Men*, directed by Sidney Lumet. Here we see Lee J. Cobb lecturing Henry Fonda, with E. G. Marshall, John Fiedler (back to camera), Edward Binns, George Voskovec, Jack Klugman, and Joseph Sweeney.

1958. Having spent several years in Europe, Orson Welles returned to America and astonished Hollywood with *Touch of Evil*, about a corrupt border cop. Heavily padded, he is seen here with Akim Tamiroff and Janet Leigh.

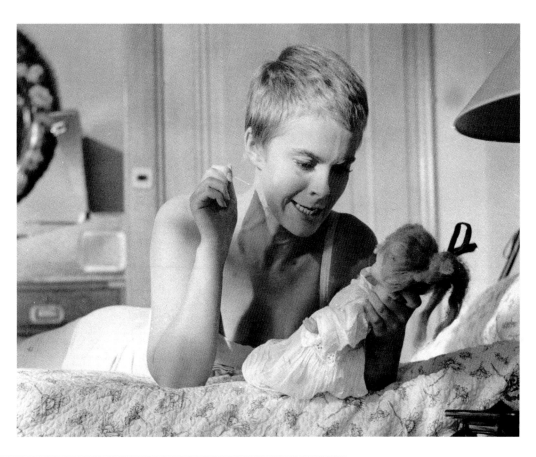

1957. Here is Jean Seberg (discovered by Otto Preminger for *Saint Joan*) in his *Bonjour Tristesse*, one of many films about troubled teenagers.

1959. *Anatomy of a Murder* was Preminger's sardonic analysis of a trial as a kind of play. This scene shows Lee Remick and George C. Scott.

333

1957. The best-selling book *Peyton Place* discovered the malaises of suburbia. The movie that followed was as big a hit—Hope Lange is seen here withLana Turner *(right)*.

1957. Deborah Kerr was a stalwart of the 1950s: *from Edward, My Son* (1949) to *The Sundowners* (1960), she was nominated six times. One of them was for John Huston's *Heaven Knows, Mr. Allison*, which she made with Robert Mitchum *(below)*.

1958. Producer-director Stanley Kramer took on many big subjects, notably race relations. In *The Defiant Ones*, Sidney Poitier and Tony Curtis are escaped convicts, shackled together *(left)*.

1959. Kramer tried the end of the world in adapting Nevil Shute's apocalyptic novel, *On the Beach.* In this off-set photo *(below)* Gregory Peck and Ava Gardner rest between scenes—or are they playing musical chairs?

1960s

1960s

Censorship Hangs Loose

America began the 1960s with a president who loved movies, whose father had made them, and who commanded the screen with his hip style. He was dead before the seismic changes of the decade that saw the battle for civil rights, turmoil on the campuses, drug culture, a sexual revolution and the end of censorship, and then Vietnam.

The movies responded—with language, nudity, sexual behavior, and attitude. There were throwbacks still, like *Cleopatra*, so costly it nearly destroyed 20th Century Fox, and there were reassuring crowd-pleasers like *My Fair Lady, West Side Story, Mary Poppins*, and *The Sound of Music.* But for most people, the 1960s exploded in 1967—and *Bonnie and Clyde* was the vital movie that took an old genre, enlivened it with sex, violence, and anti-authoritarianism, and made it play for a new generation.

Bonnie and Clyde belonged to Arthur Penn and Warren Beatty, filmmakers typical of the new age—resolved to ignore studio caution, drawn to dangerous material, and counting on the young audience. Their colleagues would be Dustin Hoffman, Mike Nichols, Robert Redford, Sidney Poitier, Faye Dunaway, Paul Newman, Steve McQueen, John Frankenheimer, Jane Fonda, Natalie Wood, Stanley Kubrick, and Barbra Streisand.

Above all, American institutions and clichés were being challenged in films as varied as *Psycho, Hud, The Apartment, 2001, To Kill a Mockingbird, In the Heat of the Night, Midnight Cowboy,* and *The Graduate.* Then, at the decade's end, along came a sleeper, made by new kids Dennis Hopper, Peter Fonda, and Jack Nicholson—but a huge hit and trendsetter—*Easy Rider.*

1960. Psycho was a film about
Phoenix, Arizona, the highway, a
modern motel, and this strange
Gothic house up on the hill
(above). As ever, Hitchcock
revealed his story through décor
and design, and audiences knew
that finally they were going to
have to enter that dread house.

1960. The decade began
famously with screams and a
terrible warning about showers.
This is Janet Leigh in *Psycho
(left)*—in many ways the
beginning of modern horror
and a climax of Hitch's mixed
feelings about voyeurism.

1960. The scream meets the
smothered mouth: Anthony
Perkins as Norman Bates in
Psycho (right)—a new kind of
villain, and one we can't help
liking . . . or perhaps even
understanding.

1963. In the small northern Californian town of Bodega Bay, Tippi Hedren and Rod Taylor make their way through devastation in a parable about the end of the world, as made by *The Birds (left)*.

1963. In *The Birds*, Hitchcock taught us to see feathered creatures differently. Here he is, on the set *(right)*, gleefully arranging the seagulls.

1964. Tippi Hedren was Hitchcock's last great discovery— and his final infatuation. She listens intently to his direction on the set of *Marnie (left)*, in which she costarred with Sean Connery—the new rage from Britain.

343

1960s

1960. Hollywood put its trust in epics. *The Magnificent Seven* was a hit western, taken from Akira Kurosawa's Japanese classic, *Seven Samurai*. Here are the seven *(right):* Yul Brynner, Steve McQueen, Horst Bucholtz, Charles Bronson, Robert Vaughn, Brad Dexter, and James Coburn.

1960. John Wayne mounted his own epic, *The Alamo (left),* in which he was Davy Crockett. Richard Widmark (holding rifle) played Jim Bowie, and Laurence Harvey (in gray cutaway jacket) was Colonel Travis. The picture did well, but the Duke was disappointed at the Oscars, where *The Apartment* beat out *The Alamo.*

1960. This is John Wayne at the turn of the decade *(right),* a mature, weather-beaten man and a naturally eloquent actor. He would find young challengers on campuses in the 1960s stronger than those he faced on the screen. But it is easier now to appreciate his grace, his skill, and the Western ideals he stood for.

1960. Producer-director Stanley Kramer delivered *Inherit the Wind*, a fictional account of the 1925 Scopes "Monkey Trial"—the great battle between evolution and religion fought between William Jennings Bryan and Clarence Darrow. It opposed two master actors—Spencer Tracy and Fredric March—with the fine character actor, Harry Morgan, as their judge *(right)*.

1961. Kramer moved on to the Holocaust in *Judgment at Nuremberg*. The film felt old-fashioned, but audiences were held by the all-star cast that included Montgomery Clift and Judy Garland in small parts, along with Spencer Tracy, Marlene Dietrich, Burt Lancaster and, as seen here, Maximilian Schell (Best Actor) and Richard Widmark in the leads *(left)*.

1960. That old-time religion flourished again in *Elmer Gantry*, taken from the Sinclair Lewis novel about evangelism. Richard Brooks directed and Burt Lancaster *(right)* won his Oscar as the preacher.

1961. Movie musicals were gone, but there were still films that adapted stage shows. Natalie Wood didn't sing as Maria in *West Side Story (left)*, but she was vital to the film's commercial success. The former child and teenage actress would be an essential star—and a beloved figure—in the 1960s, brave enough to take on some very daring material.

1961. How do you codirect? Jerome Robbins and Robert Wise needed a two-seat crane *(right)*. They shared credit on *West Side Story* and helped the picture to ten Oscars, including Best Picture and Best Direction.

1961. Here is Rita Moreno (on the way to her supporting actress Oscar) in *West Side Story (left)*, with songs by Leonard Bernstein and choreography by Jerome Robbins.

1962. *Lawrence of Arabia* and director David Lean were both English. But the picture was produced by Sam Spiegel and Columbia and it was a huge international success. In this still Anthony Quinn is a Bedouin chieftain protecting his water rights *(left)*.

1962. Peter O'Toole relaxing between scenes during the filming of *Lawrence of Arabia (left). Lawrence* won Best Picture and another six Oscars. But O'Toole was overlooked (the Oscar went to Gregory Peck in *To Kill a Mockingbird*)—the first of seven nominations without a win.

1962. Peter O'Toole and David Lean during the long, very difficult desert location shooting on *Lawrence of Arabia (right).* It's part of the power of the film that the hero and the actor were so deeply mixed, and confused, in Lawrence.

1962. Darryl F. Zanuck returned from retirement to produce *The Longest Day*—his mammoth account of D-Day, 1944. The all-star cast included Robert Mitchum *(right),* Richard Burton, Henry Fonda, Rod Steiger, and John Wayne.

THE GREATEST ROMANCE AND ADVENTURE IN A THOUSAND YEARS!

SAMUEL BRONSTON presents
CHARLTON HESTON and SOPHIA LOREN in EL CID

It's the story of one of the world's greatest heroes...magnificently produced in Spain where he lived, loved and fought!

RAF VALLONE · GENEVIEVE PAGE
co-starring JOHN FRASER · GARY RAYMOND · HURD HATFIELD · MASSIMO SERATO and HERBERT LOM
music by MIKLOS ROZSA written by FREDRIC M. FRANK and PHILIP YORDAN directed by ANTHONY MANN
70 mm SUPER TECHNIRAMA· TECHNICOLOR® a SAMUEL BRONSTON PRODUCTION in cooperation with DEAR FILM PRODUCTIONS distributed by ALLIED ARTISTS

1961. Producer Samuel Bronston moved his operation to Spain and had a great hit with *El Cid (left).* The eleventh-century epic starred Charlton Heston as a Castillian knight and Sophia Loren as his ladylove, and the battles were in the hands of that master of the Western, director Anthony Mann.

1963. But Bronston's empire foundered with a story about the 1900 Boxer Rebellion: *55 Days at Peking,* the last film by Nicholas Ray. In this on-set photo *(right)* Ray directs Flora Robson as the dowager Empress.

1961. There was also a world of smaller, darker films—the swan song of black-and-white. *Shadows (right)*, written and directed by actor John Cassavetes, was shot on 16mm for only $40,000. It was an important art-house success—starring Anthony Ray (the son of Nicholas) and Lelia Goldoni.

1961. *The Hustler* was the first film to see what a cinematic game pool could be. It was a comeback for director Robert Rossen, and proof that Paul Newman *(below)* was now a leading star.

1961. Elia Kazan was widely regarded as the greatest director of actors. Here we see him (in a white cap) rehearsing a group that includes Warren Beatty and Natalie Wood (in head scarf) for *Splendor in the Grass (left)*.

1961. *Splendor in the Grass* showed that Natalie Wood had grown up *(below)*. It also introduced Warren Beatty as a male star. Under the direction of Elia Kazan, it also suggested that sexual candor might be a subject of the 1960s—or a revolution.

1962. Joan Crawford and Bette Davis in the same film? Robert Aldrich brought them together to play sisters in *What Ever Happened to Baby Jane?* Their fans were shocked, and most of Hollywood winced at the world's new, cynical attitude. The garish color of this promotional still reflects the movie's harsh black-and-white look.

1962. Not since *The Lost Weekend* had anyone done alcoholism as well as *Days of Wine and Roses*. Blake Edwards directed, and Jack Lemmon and Lee Remick were the afflicted couple.

1962. Taken from the novel by Richard Condon and directed by John Frankenheimer, *The Manchurian Candidate* introduced a sense of paranoia to politics. It's the story of a mother and son, and here Angela Lansbury is about to plant a controversial kiss on Laurence Harvey's lips. Don't miss the Queen of Diamonds.

1962. Arthur Penn had directed *The Miracle Worker* (the story of Helen Keller's childhood) on stage. When he transferred it to film, with Anne Bancroft and Patty Duke, the result was so powerful that both actresses won Oscars.

1963. *Hud* **was a tough modern** Western, set in Texas ranching country. Martin Ritt directed. Paul Newman played a heel and Patricia Neal walked off with the supporting actress award.

1964. Just before his death, Robert Rossen made *Lilith*, a film about madness in which Jean Seberg gave her finest performance, and Warren Beatty was her love-stricken nurse *(right)*. A flop in its day, it now seems like one of the most daring films of the 1960s.

1966. Beatty went further into the experimental in Arthur Penn's *Mickey One (below)*, playing a nightclub entertainer who believes he is being hounded by the Mob.

1968. John Cassavetes's *Faces* was a long, semi-improvised study of broken lives, marriage, and lies. It starred Gena Rowlands *(left),* who would be the leading player in the director's work—as well as his wife.

1967. In *The Graduate,* Mike Nichols caught the plight of the young man who has lost all faith in the world he has been educated for. It was a comedy, but the sexual intrigue was shocking. Newcomer Dustin Hoffman gazes at a leg belonging to Anne Bancroft *(below).*

1962. In John Frankenheimer's *Birdman of Alcatraz,* Burt Lancaster played Robert Stroud— the true story of a hardened criminal who became an authority on birds while serving a long sentence in the San Francisco prison.

1966. Arthur Penn's *The Chase* concerned mob instincts in a Southern town. Robert Redford was the escaped convict who comes back to see his girl (Jane Fonda) while Marlon Brando was the sheriff who protects him against the mob. It was a further sign that no one had a more anguished sense of violence than Penn. Here are Brando and Redford in a moment from the film *(left).*

1967. Robert Aldrich's *The Dirty Dozen* involved convicted criminals being trained for a special military mission to be carried out on D-Day eve. Yet again, the code was being squeezed. This on-set photo captured John Cassavetes and Lee Marvin shooting a scene together.

1967. *Cool Hand Luke* was a new sort of prison film. In the notorious egg-eating scene *(left)*, Paul Newman is attended by George Kennedy, who won the supporting actor Oscar.

1960. "I am Spartacus" was the great line in the movie, yet everyone knew that Spartacus was Kirk Douglas *(right)*—that he was the star and the producer, and the man in charge.

1960. In fact, Douglas fired his first director, Anthony Mann, and replaced him with the young Stanley Kubrick (they had met on *Paths of Glory*). Kirk rehearses a fight scene with Woody Strode *(below)* while Kubrick (seated and obscured on the lower right) looks on.

1962. Could it be filmed?
Vladimir Nabokov's story was set in America, but Stanley Kubrick chose to make *Lolita* in England. James Mason was Humbert Humbert and Sue Lyon was just a few years older than Nabokov had intended *(left)*. With this film Kubrick became a resident of England.

1964. Another Kubrick movie shot in England, *Dr. Strangelove or: How I Learned to Stop Worrying and Love the Bomb* still felt like an American film. Here is Kubrick, a former still photographer, lining up a shot *(below)* that involves Sterling Hayden and Peter Sellers (who played three roles in the picture).

1968. *2001*, filmed entirely in Britain, took years of preparation and the design of new equipment. Nothing before it had so perfectly captured the timelessness and weightlessness of space *(above)*. But *2001* had meaning, too, and audiences talked about it all over the world.

1968. Here is Keir Dullea as one of the astronauts *(right)*— but many people felt that HAL, the computer, was the film's best character.

1968. Using special effects hitherto undreamed of, and working from Arthur C. Clarke's book, Kubrick greeted the space age with its first spacey film— *2001: A Space Odyssey*. Kubrick is crouched over the camera *(left)*, laying out a scene—*2001* was the project that made clear his determination to be slow, perfect, and completely in control.

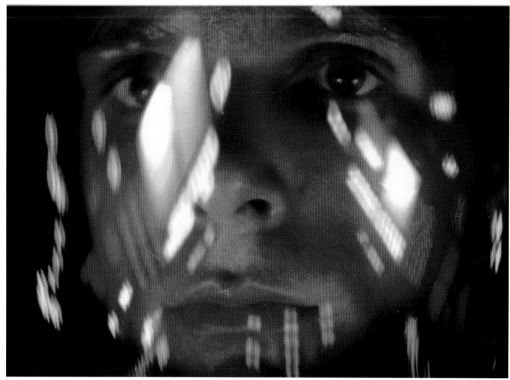

1960s

1964. Disney decided to film *Mary Poppins,* the P. L. Travers book about a perfect nanny in early twentieth-century London—and Julie Andrews made her screen debut in the role *(right).* The result was one of the great hits of the decade, and the beginning of a move at Disney to develop films for both children and adults.

1965. Then Fox took on the Rodgers and Hammerstein stage hit, *The Sound of Music.* In this on-set photo, Julie Andrews rehearses a number in one of the Austrian landscapes chosen by director Robert Wise *(left).* The film won five Oscars, including Best Director and Best Picture.

1964. On New York and London stages, Julie Andrews had been Eliza Doolittle in *My Fair Lady.* For the movie, however, Warners felt they needed a bigger name—so Audrey Hepburn got the nod (with Marni Nixon singing her songs) and Rex Harrison reprised Henry Higgins *(right).* Directed by George Cukor and dressed by Cecil Beaton, the film was a hit. But they didn't know that Julie Andrews was about to become a star.

1960. If Julie Andrews was the perfect nanny for the age, Elizabeth Taylor was the dream tramp. *Butterfield 8 (left)* was one of her poorest films, but it won Taylor her first Oscar—largely because she had just survived serious illness in the build-up to *Cleopatra*.

1961. Once upon a time, *Cleopatra* was a simple little epic, to be produced by Walter Wanger, directed by Rouben Mamoulian and filmed in England. In those days Liz was married to singer Eddie Fisher. Here they are on an Egyptian set, with Mr. Wanger *(right)*.

1963. But Liz fell ill. London turned into Rome. Wanger and Mamoulian gave way to Darryl Zanuck and Joseph L. Mankiewicz. And Liz met Richard Burton. The romance and the scandal that followed were an ocean on which the film floated like a barge the size of a canoe. Forty-four million dollars later, the film finally opened *(left)*.

1966. Burton and Taylor became a hyphenate for headlines. But they were also daring actors—never more so than in Edward Albee's *Who's Afraid of Virginia Woolf?*, the directorial debut of Mike Nichols, and the basis for Taylor's second Oscar. In this scene still Taylor is restrained from attacking Burton by George Segal; Sandy Dennis is on lower right.

1967. Taylor became a very serious actress, and joined with Marlon Brando in John Huston's film of Carson McCullers's story of betrayal on a military post in the South, *Reflections in a Golden Eye.*

1962. One of the most beloved dramas of the era was *To Kill a Mockingbird*, directed by Robert Mulligan from the Harper Lee novel, and produced by Alan J. Pakula. Gregory Peck won his Oscar as lawyer Atticus Finch—seen here questioning Brock Peters.

1962. In *Cape Fear*, Peck was the husband and father threatened by Robert Mitchum. There were undertones of sex and violence in the film that grated against the limits set by censorship.

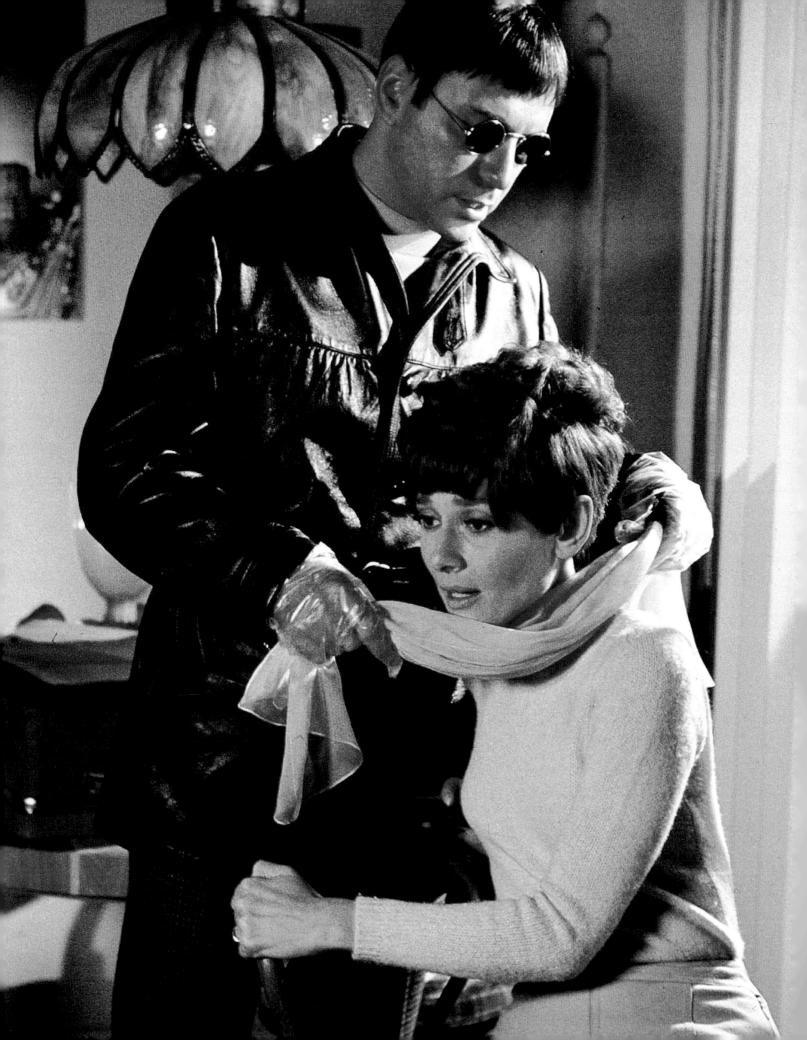

1967. Truman Capote's
documentary novel, *In Cold Blood*, about murders in Kansas, was faithfully filmed by Richard Brooks, with Robert Blake and Scott Wilson as the killers. John Forsythe, *center*, was the police detective on the case *(left)*.

1967. It had worked on stage
and it worked on screen. Frederick Knott's play, *Wait Until Dark (left)*, directed by Terence Young, had Audrey Hepburn as the blind woman threatened by Alan Arkin and his thugs who are searching for heroin.

1968. Real-life crime again
in the form of *The Boston Strangler*—a bold departure for Tony Curtis, and a film that asked the audience to understand a psychotic killer, seen here with one of his victims, Sally Kirkland *(right)*. To get the part, Curtis disguised his hair, eyebrows, eyelashes, and nose, and sent the makeover photos to director Richard Fleischer—who did not realize that they were Curtis. The film was the first to use multi-screen imagery.

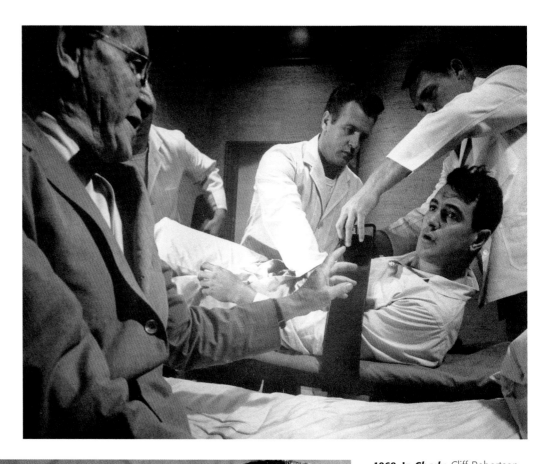

1966. *Seconds* **means** what it says—it's about a second chance at life. Directed by John Frankenheimer, it is one of the scariest films of the time. Will Gere is shown here spreading sweet words as Rock Hudson is strapped down for his "operation" *(right)*.

1968. In *Charly,* Cliff Robertson won an Oscar playing a mildly retarded man who has experimental brain surgery and becomes a genius—and then regresses. Ralph Nelson directed. Robertson tries to decipher a maze *(left)* with Lilia Skala.

1968. Witchcraft hardly seemed modern, or likely, in New York. But Roman Polanski turned the Ira Levin novel, *Rosemary's Baby*, into a deeply disturbing film, with Mia Farrow as the haunted young mother, and Ruth Gordon in an outstanding turn as the next-door neighbor *(right)*.

1968. The classic McQueen role was as the San Francisco cop in *Bullitt (left)*, directed by Englishman Peter Yates. The steep streets and sharp corners of that city helped one of the screen's all-time best car-chase scenes—with McQueen doing his own driving.

1963. Steve McQueen was one of the great stars of the 1960s. A hit in *The Magnificent Seven*, he would be one of the prisoners-of-war in John Sturges's *The Great Escape*—in the course of which he was indulged in a lengthy solo scene for man and motorcycle *(left)*.

1968. McQueen was tough, laconic, and down-to-earth, but he went beyond his ordinary range as the brilliant thief in *The Thomas Crown Affair*. This is the scene where he and Faye Dunaway discover the erotic subtext in chess *(right)*.

1963. In Ralph Nelson's *Lilies of the Field*, Sidney Poitier played a handyman who helps some nuns build a chapel *(right)*, and became the first black actor to win a leading-part Oscar. More than that, Poitier was an authentic star.

1967. Poitier was the surprise guest in Stanley Kramer's *Guess Who's Coming to Dinner?* which also starred Katharine Houghton (Katharine Hepburn's niece), Spencer Tracy (in his last role), and Katharine Hepburn. Kramer, in short sleeves, directs the action *(left)*.

1967. Poitier costarred with Rod Steiger in Norman Jewison's *In the Heat of the Night (right)*. They played a big city detective and a Southern redneck sheriff. This time Steiger won the Oscar.

1960. One of the most influential dark comedies of the 1960s was Billy Wilder's *The Apartment (left),* with Shirley MacLaine and Jack Lemmon. It was a portrait of the small corruptions of ordinary life that won ten nominations and five Oscars (including Best Picture, Best Direction, and Best Story and Screenplay).

1962. The film *Gypsy,* directed by Mervyn LeRoy, came from the stage show about Gypsy Rose Lee and her mother, Rose Hovick. In the movie, Natalie Wood was the kid who stripped *(left),* and Rosalind Russell was Mama.

1963. Launched by Stanley Kubrick, Peter Sellers became an international star—typically as the bumbling Inspector Clouseau in *The Pink Panther* series, directed by Blake Edwards *(right).*

1961. Blake Edwards' film of *Breakfast at Tiffany's* wasn't as sour as the Truman Capote novella. But the film had two things on its side: Audrey Hepburn as Holly Golightly (seen here with George Peppard) and the song, "Moon River," by Henry Mancini and Johnny Mercer.

1963. Audrey Hepburn had another great success in the romantic thriller, *Charade*, directed by Stanley Donen. How could it fail when her costar was Cary Grant—in his penultimate picture?

1967. _The Producers_ was a sardonic satire on show business that introduced the Mel Brooks touch. Here we see Gene Wilder, Zero Mostel (who wants to produce a flop) and Lee Meredith. It's a nice reminder in the year 2001 that the original movie was not a big hit.

1968. Another hit transfer, stage-to-screen, involved the Neil Simon play, _The Odd Couple_, about ill-matched guys (fusspot and slob) who end up living together. Gene Saks directed and Walter Matthau and Jack Lemmon worked their undoubted chemistry.

1960s

1962. Seventy-six trombones and an awful lot of people went into the making of *The Music Man.* Here, producer-director Morton DaCosta (*center right,* in glasses and striped short-sleeved shirt), works with Shirley Jones and Hermione Gingold.

1967. *Doctor Dolittle* turned out to be a big flop for Fox, but it demonstrated how far Rex Harrison (in the fourth decade of his career) had become a major movie star. He won the Oscar for *My Fair Lady* and he was nominated for his Caesar in *Cleopatra.*

1968. They said it was just a matter of time and the right vehicle—and they were right. Hailed as the singer of her age, Barbra Streisand won the Oscar in her screen debut, playing Fanny Brice in *Funny Girl* (directed by the veteran William Wyler).

1969. Streisand came back in *Hello Dolly!*, directed by Gene Kelly. In this still she belts out the title song with Louis Armstrong, the jazz genius who had his biggest hit record with the song.

1969. Bob Fosse's *Sweet Charity* was a musical derived from the Federico Fellini film, *Le Notti di Cabiria* (1957). The camera captured Paula Kelly, Shirley MacLaine and Chita Rivera in midair, doing the number, "There's Gotta be Something Better than This."

1960s

1960. Roger Corman directed
himself, and he gave chances
to newcomers—like Coppola,
Scorsese, and Bogdanovich. He
was best known for a series of
mock horror films that usually
starred Vincent Price—this is
The Fall of the House of Usher
(right), with Myrna Fahey.

1963. Never mind the dreadful
remake, the original *The*
Haunting was everything the title
promised. Robert Wise directed
the adaptation of Shirley Jackson's
1959 book. In a bird's-eye shot
(below), three members of the
team investigating the supposedly
haunted Hill House—Russ
Tamblyn, Claire Bloom and
Richard Johnson—look upward,
wondering what that noise was.

1965. David Lean took on Boris Pasternak's novel, *Doctor Zhivago (left)*. He might have won Best Picture again—with Julie Christie and Omar Sharif as his leads—but he ran up against *The Sound of Music*.

1968. There was a twenty-five-year age gap, but in *The Lion in Winter*, Peter O'Toole and Katharine Hepburn played king and queen *(below)*. He got one of his nominations, and she won her fourth Oscar—a record she still holds.

PARAMOUNT PICTURES presents
A DINO DE LAURENTIIS PRODUCTION

JANE FONDA

The space age adventuress whose sex-ploits are among the most bizarre ever seen.

SEE

BARBARELLA

DO HER THING!

STARRING

JOHN PHILLIP LAW · MARCEL MARCEAU

SPECIAL GUEST APPEARANCE

DAVID HEMMINGS AS DILDANO UGO TOGNAZZI AS MARK HAND

PRODUCED BY
DINO DE LAURENTIIS

DIRECTED BY
ROGER VADIM

Lyrics and Music by Bob Crewe and Charles Fox · Performed by
The Bob Crewe Generation Orchestra Available on Dynavoice Records

FROM THE BEST SELLER 'BARBARELLA'
BY JEAN CLAUDE FOREST
PUBLISHED BY 'LE TERRAIN VAGUE'

SCREENPLAY BY
TERRY SOUTHERN

A FRANCO-ITALIAN CO-PRODUCTION · DINO DE LAURENTIIS · CINEMATOGRAFICA S.p.A. · MARIANNE PRODUCTIONS · PANAVISION® TECHNICOLOR®

SUGGESTED FOR MATURE AUDIENCES

1968. Franklin J. Schaffner launched a cult following with *Planet of the Apes*, based on Pierre Boulle's early 1960s sci-fi novel of a world where savage humans are enslaved by civilized apes. In this off-set photo *(above)*, a few of the savages and masters engage in a little poker during a break in filming.

1968. Charlton Heston (seen in the film poster, *right*) was the lead, playing an astronaut who lands on the planet. Roddy McDowall and Kim Hunter sat through hours of makeup to become sensitive chimp scientists.

1968. *Barbarella* was a French sci-fi strip cartoon, brought to the screen by Roger Vadim and given sex appeal by Vadim's wife at the time—Jane Fonda *(left)*. Fonda was increasingly outspoken politically, but she was shaping up as an important actress.

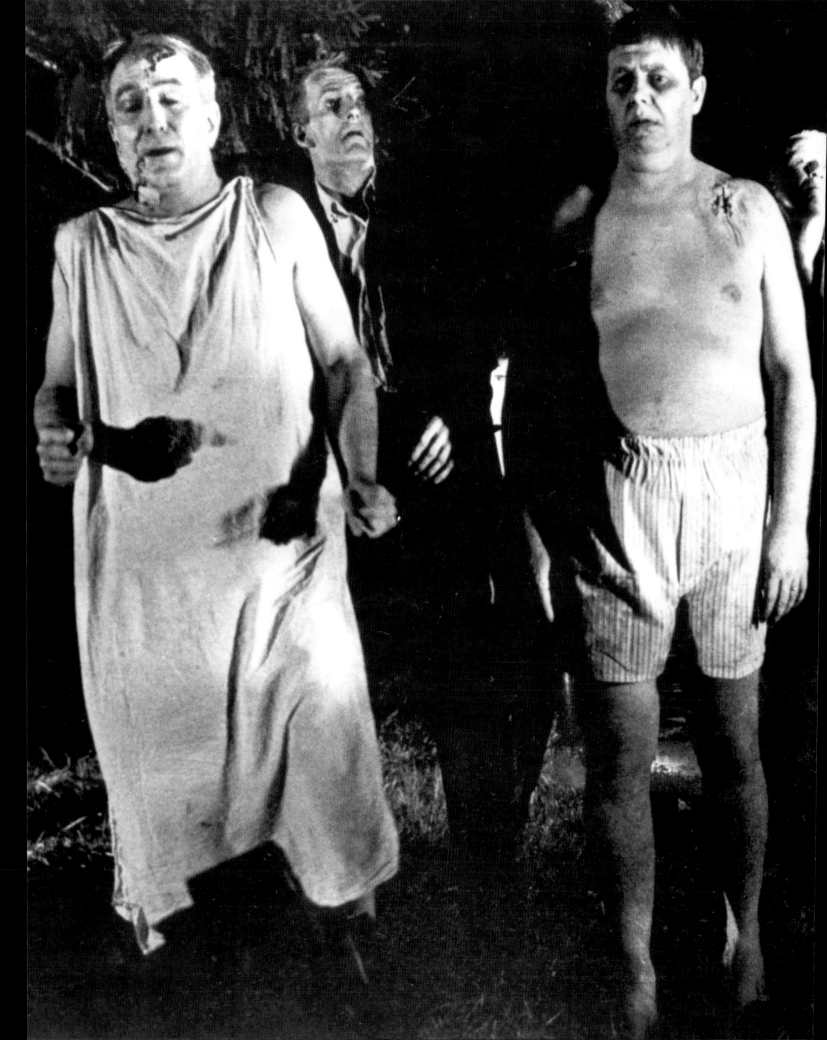

1968. On a shoestring budget,
George Romero revolutionized
the horror film with *Night of
the Living Dead,* in which the
good guys are threatened by
flesh-eating zombies. The people
here *(left)* are not the good guys.

1968. *Night of the Living Dead*
was made outside the system—
in Pittsburgh—but its profit ratio
was an inspiration to franchises
that followed, like *Halloween,
Nightmare on Elm Street,* and
Friday the 13th. One of the
original posters *(above),* sets
the graphic tone of the film.

1967. It was a crucial year, in large part because of *Bonnie and Clyde*, an extraordinary fusion of the gangster genre with the mood of the rebellious America of the late 1960s. It was violent, it was sexy and, eventually, it was a smash hit. Arthur Penn directed. Warren Beatty produced, and he and Faye Dunaway were the beautiful young killers *(right)*.

1967. There was also *Point Blank*, a fascinating, dream-like film noir, full of sex and violence, with Lee Marvin like a sleepwalker in search of the $93,000 owed to him by the Mob. It was directed by a young Englishman, John Boorman. Marvin is seen here with Sharon Acker *(left)*.

1969. William Goldman wrote the script (and won an Oscar for it) and George Roy Hill directed— *Butch Cassidy and the Sundance Kid (right)* was a wistful, parody Western. Its enormous popular success owed a lot to the teaming of Paul Newman and Robert Redford; Katharine Ross was their partner in love and crime.

1960s

1965. *Cat Ballou* **was a comedy** Western that marked the stardom of a former supporting actor—Lee Marvin—and the arrival of a newcomer, Jane Fonda, who had also drawn attention in *Barbarella*.

1966. In Richard Brooks's western *The Professionals,* a group of men (including Lee Marvin and Burt Lancaster) are hired to recover a man's kidnapped wife. It's only late in the day that they discover how happy the wife was to be taken.

1969. Henry Hathaway's *True Grit* was an old-fashioned throwback of a Western, but it won an Oscar for John Wayne—seen here with Kim Darby and Glen Campbell.

1969. The extreme opposite of *True Grit*, Sam Peckinpah's *The Wild Bunch* was a notoriously violent film that depicted the West as a struggle between rough integrity and corrupt progress. Peckinpah is photographed rehearsing with William Holden, who gave a superb performance as the leader of the Bunch.

1960s

1969. *Easy Rider*
(*previous pages*) was a nearly
experimental film, made very
cheaply and codirected by
Dennis Hopper and Peter Fonda.
It was a road film and a drug
film, and above all it was a
celebration of the new young
generation. It made a fortune
and changed the movies.

1969. *Easy Rider* **also
demonstrated** the appeal, the
wit and the lazy, lethal charm of
an actor named Jack Nicholson—
a force still active in the best
American cinema. Nicholson
meets up with Fonda in a still
from the film (*right*).

1969. *Midnight Cowboy* got an
X rating because of sex and
language—but it still won Best
Picture. So many barriers were
broken in John Schlesinger's
film, though the homosexual
link between Dustin Hoffman
and Jon Voight (*left*) was still
treated gently.

1969. Derived from a wonderful,
bleak novel by Horace McCoy,
They Shoot Horses, Don't They
was an uncompromisingly
pessimistic film about a
marathon dance contest in the
1930s. Sydney Pollack directed
an ensemble cast that included
Jane Fonda and Michael Sarrazin
(*right*), as well as Bruce Dern,
Susannah York, Red Buttons,
Bonnie Bedelia, and Gig Young.

1969. The image that said it all about sex and society *(above)*: Elliott Gould, Natalie Wood, Robert Culp, and Dyan Cannon in Paul Mazursky's *Bob & Carol & Ted & Alice*.

1969. Maybe the most vital new face and voice at the decade's end was Woody Allen. He was known as a stand-up comic and a writer, but now he began to direct—with *Take the Money and Run*. Allen was also the movie's star *(right)*.

1967. It was awful, but people loved it—after all, the whole concept of "bad movies we love" was coming into being. *Valley of the Dolls* came from a Jacqueline Susann novel, and starred Barbara Parkin, Sharon Tate, and Patty Duke as forlorn babes in showbiz *(left)*.

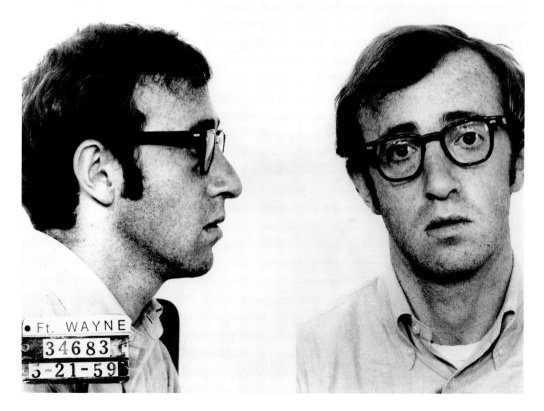

1970s

1970s

The Silver Age

Hollywood was staggering in 1970. The studios made TV, not movies. Film had lost its pioneers, and was short of confidence and audience allegiance. Ironically, this helped admit a generation of exciting filmmakers. So the early 1970s now seems like a moment of great films that explored the true nature of America with new intensity.

There was Francis Ford Coppola, with the first two parts of *The Godfather*— and an example to others like Martin Scorsese *(Taxi Driver)*, Robert Altman *(Nashville, McCabe and Mrs Miller)*, Bob Rafelson *(Five Easy Pieces)*, William Friedkin *(The French Connection)*, Alan J. Pakula *(Klute)*, Hal Ashby *(Shampoo)*, Peter Bogdanovich *(The Last Picture Show)*, Roman Polanski *(Chinatown)*, and Woody Allen *(Annie Hall)*.

It was the age when film studies became a college staple. Critics like Pauline Kael and Andrew Sarris became national figures. There was an audience eager to discover the classics of Hollywood's past as well as the best foreign films.

Then along came two directors with fantasies that helped the picture business regain confidence.

Steven Spielberg's *Jaws* and George Lucas's *Star Wars* stressed kid audiences and mass openings, the films backed up by toys and merchandise. Hollywood took heart. A fresh generation of lawyers and agents ran the show. And the studios began to be bought out by large international conglomerates.

But at the end of the decade, there was still so much to admire: *Rocky*, making a Cinderella out of Sylvester Stallone; *One Flew Over the Cuckoo's Nest; Network; All the President's Men; The Deer Hunter;* and Coppola's third masterpiece, *Apocalypse Now.*

1970. A decade marked by turmoil in the young began with a charmingly old-fashioned celebration of young love (and never having to say sorry): it's Arthur Hiller's *Love Story* (taken from the Erich Segal novel), with newcomers Ryan O'Neal and Ali McGraw *(right)*.

1973. *The Paper Chase* was a film about the pressures at Harvard Law School, written and directed by James Bridges, and establishing long-time producer John Houseman as an actor (he won Best Supporting Actor as the tough law professor). Things get rocky for Timothy Bottoms when he falls in love with the teacher's daughter, Lindsay Wagner *(left)*.

1970. *Little Big Man* (adapted from Thomas Berger's novel) was an Arthur Penn Western that retold the story of Custer and the Sioux as a parable of Vietnam. It was a huge step forward in cinema's recognition of Native Americans, and a very violent film. This is a scene with Amy Eccles and Dustin Hoffman *(right)*, who played a character who lived to be over 100.

1970. *Airport* was another throwback—some people called it *Grand Hotel* in an airliner. But it was a big hit (even if it seemed primed for later parodies). There's trouble in the air and Dean Martin and Jacqueline Bisset are trying to restore calm *(right)*.

1972. Disaster films became very popular—notably *The Poseidon Adventure*, in which a cruise ship turns upside down. The film was directed by English veteran Ronald Neame, and the all-star cast included Gene Hackman (crawling up the ladder, *left*) and Shelley Winters.

1974. *The Towering Inferno* was based on the new fear of high-rise buildings on fire. But as a movie it was the old disaster recipe, with a lot of stars tossed in—like Steve McQueen as the fire chief *(right)*.

1970. It was President Nixon's favorite film (as well as Best Picture) in the dark days of Vietnam—which shows how bold and controversial *Patton* was. George C. Scott was tremendous as the flawed general, but he declined to accept his Oscar. Franklin Schaffner directed, and the screenplay Oscar was shared between Edmund H. North and a young man named Francis Ford Coppola.

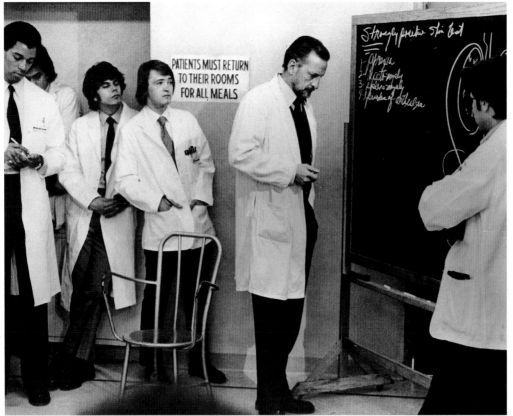

1971. The new unease with American institutions was typified by *The Hospital*, a fiery diatribe against chaos in the health system, written by Paddy Chayefsky and directed by Arthur Hiller. George C. Scott played a doctor at the end of his tether.

1972. Jack Lemmon won his best actor Oscar in a startling little film, *Save the Tiger*, directed by John G. Avildsen, about the decline of an American hero. It was one more sign of the new social candor in our pictures.

1974. Director Paul Mazursky made a number of small, personal comedies. In *Harry and Tonto*, Art Carney won the Oscar playing an old man who travels across country with his cat.

1970s

1971. One of the brilliant newcomers in the 1970s was former critic Peter Bogdanovich. His *The Last Picture Show* was a slice of Texas life, notable for its black-and-white photography, its subtle, humane style, and a superb ensemble cast that included Ellen Burstyn and Cybill Shepherd *(right)*.

1972. Bogdanovich followed up with a real screwball comedy, *What's Up, Doc? (left)*, a riot of invention, with Ryan O'Neal and Barbra Streisand inviting comparison with Cary Grant and Katharine Hepburn in *Bringing Up Baby*.

1973. With *Paper Moon*, Bogdanovich made it three in a row. This was a delightful comedy about con men, set in the 1930s, with Ryan O'Neal allowing himself to be upstaged and outwitted by his own daughter, Tatum *(right)*.

Where does the camping trip end...

and the nightmare begin...?

Deliverance

A JOHN BOORMAN FILM Starring **JON VOIGHT · BURT REYNOLDS** in "DELIVERANCE" x
Co-Starring NED BEATTY·RONNY COX · Screenplay by James Dickey Based on his novel · Produced and Directed by John Boorman
PANAVISION®· TECHNICOLOR®·From Warner Bros., A Warner Communications Company WB Released by Columbia-Warner Distributors Ltd.

1972. Englishman John Boorman went to the rural South to make *Deliverance*, a very scary picture about civilized man reverting to primitive nature. The brilliant poster *(above)* was an inspiration for the ad campaign on *Jaws*.

1973. *Soylent Green* was a sci-fi prediction about New York in 2022, where the masses are fed a product called Soylent Green. Charlton Heston—still an ideal heroic figure—plays a cop who discovers that the foodstuff is definitely not made from soy *(left)*. Richard Fleischer directed.

1973. *The Exorcist* comes to call. The scariest film of the decade had Max von Sydow as the exorcist *(right)*, Linda Blair as the child victim, and Ellen Burstyn as her mother. William Friedkin directed the movie.

1970. BBS was a new company that grew out of the *Easy Rider* success. Its aim was low-budget movies that explored the real America. One of their hits was *Five Easy Pieces*, directed by Bob Rafelson, in which Jack Nicholson (seen here with Karen Black) played an oil-rigger trying to escape his artistic family.

1971. In *Carnal Knowledge*, another great American institution—sexual confidence—was undermined. Cartoonist Jules Feiffer adapted his own play and Mike Nichols directed. By now, Jack Nicholson was almost inevitable as one of the male leads, but everyone was surprised by the depth of Ann-Margret's performance.

1972. Working for BBS and Bob Rafelson again, Jack Nicholson and Bruce Dern played brothers in *The King of Marvin Gardens*—the one introvert, creative, depressed; the other extrovert, conman, and crazy. They are seen here with Julia Anne Robinson.

1973. Next Nicholson did a film written by an old friend, Robert Towne. *The Last Detail* followed the adventures of two sailors escorting a third to prison. Hal Ashby directed: here we see the central trio—Otis Young, Randy Quaid, and Nicholson *(left)*.

421

1974. People were gathering around Nicholson: the role of detective Jake Gittes in *Chinatown* (seen with costar Faye Dunaway, *right*) was written specifically for him by Robert Towne. Set in the 1930s, *Chinatown* was a story about the ways in which Los Angeles found or stole the water it needed to survive.

1974. But by 1974, water meant Watergate, too, and "Chinatown" became a byword for corruption in America. Director Roman Polanski (who altered Towne's ending) is seen here rehearsing Nicholson and John Huston for the final scenes *(left)*.

1974. The heroine of *Chinatown*, and in many ways the chief victim of its intrigue, was Evelyn Mulwreay, played by Faye Dunaway *(right)*. She managed to evoke memories of the great actresses from the 1930s, while adding a very modern feeling of tragedy. The nose? You know the nose.

WATER BOND ISSUE PAS

1970s

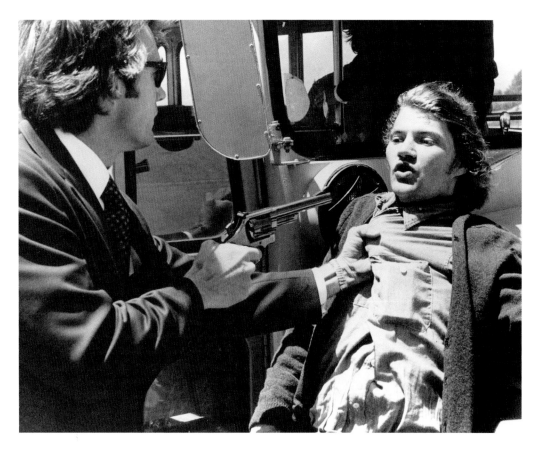

1971. Clint Eastwood emerged as another key figure of the times. In Don Siegel's *Dirty Harry*, he was a very controversial San Francisco cop driven to take the law into his own hands—and, finally, to throw away his badge in disgust. In this still Eastwood roughs up one of the loathsome villains of the era, Andy Robinson *(right)*.

1972. Eastwood also revealed himself as a very good director. In *High Plains Drifter*, he took on an enigmatic angel of death figure, clearly based on the character he had played in Sergio Leone's spaghetti Westerns. Eastwood takes a bath here assisted by Billy Curtis *(left)*, who becomes his sidekick in the film.

1976. Eastwood also directed *The Outlaw Josey Wales (right)*, after he had fired screenwriter Philip Kaufman. The poster emphasizes the guns, but in fact the Western played on irony and humor—Eastwood did not always take himself seriously.

jane fonda · donald sutherland

Lots
of guys
swing with
a call girl
like Bree.

One guy just
wants to
kill her.

an alan j. pakula production
'klute'

1971. Jane Fonda was a prevailing figure in the 1970s, and she won a new reputation for authority and ability with her Oscar-winning performance as the edgy call girl Bree Daniels, in Alan J. Pakula's *Klute*—the name of the detective, played by Donald Sutherland, who tries to save her.

1977. In *Julia*, Fonda played the great playwright Lillian Hellman. It was a story of Hellman's friendship with a European woman (played by Vanessa Redgrave) who becomes involved in the fight against Nazism. Fred Zinnemann directed.

1978. In Hal Ashby's *Coming Home*, Fonda won her second Oscar as the conservative Marine's wife who is sexually awoken by Jon Voight's paraplegic Vietnam veteran. Voight also won an Oscar in a picture that began to tell unpleasant truths about the Vietnam experience.

1979. In *The China Syndrome*, Fonda played a television reporter. The film also costarred Jack Lemmon and Michael Douglas. In turn, Douglas was its coproducer. The story of a major nuclear power station accident, the film coincided with the March 1979 incident at Three Mile Island.

1971. Young director William Friedkin felt the cop picture had gone stale. So in *The French Connection* he wanted everything more real than it had ever been. The result won Best Picture along with Oscars for Friedkin himself and Gene Hackman as the tough cop "Popeye" Doyle. With a dazzling car chase, the film involved Doyle's pursuit of a suave French drug dealer, played by Fernando Rey.

1971. The great novelty in *Shaft* was that the hero was a black man. The picture was written by Ernest Tidyman (who had also done *The French Connection*), and it was directed by Gordon Parks. Richard Roundtree played the stylish private eye, bouncing along on the memorable score by Isaac Hayes.

1972. Sam Peckinpah saw the Jim Thompson novel, *The Getaway*, as an ideal vehicle for Steve McQueen. He cast Ali McGraw as the girl—and the two fell in love on the set, which fed the tabloids and gave an extra sexual charge to their scenes together.

1974. Nothing deterred John Cassavetes from following his own course. But with *A Woman Under the Influence*, he found a mainstream audience, thanks in part to the Oscar-nominated performance of Gena Rowlands in the title role.

1972. Not many people saw it, but critics loved the realism of John Huston's boxing picture, *Fat City*, taken from Leonard Gardner's novel, and starring Stacy Keach and Jeff Bridges, seen here taking a ten count.

1973. Bruce Lee died in 1973, the year that saw the release of his greatest hit, *Enter the Dragon*, directed by Robert Clouse. Kung Fu was still a marginal genre, but Lee was the pioneer of the martial arts trend.

1973. Sam Peckinpah's *Pat Garrett and Billy the Kid* was recut by its distributor, but in later years longer versions have shown it to be one of the great, elegiac Westerns. Kris Kristofferson was the Kid and James Coburn (seen here with Richard Jaeckel, *left*) played Garrett. Bob Dylan played a small part in the film and wrote the score.

1978. *Comes a Horseman* was a Western set in the 1940s. Directed by Alan J. Pakula, it starred James Caan and Jane Fonda and included a lovely supporting performance from former stunt rider, Richard Farnsworth.

1973. *The Sting* won Best Picture because everyone loved the intricate, semicomic story of confidence tricksters in the 1930s. David S. Ward did the script, and George Roy Hill directed the reunion of Paul Newman *(left)* and Robert Redford.

1973. Redford played a floater in *The Sting*, a guy who may be double-double-crossing his partner. He's seen here with Robert Shaw *(right)*, who was magnificently gruff and stupid as the gangster.

1974. Redford also played the lead role in one of the great disappointments of the decade— Jack Clayton's *The Great Gatsby (left)*, scripted by Francis Ford Coppola, and also starring Mia Farrow as Gatsby's beloved.

1970s

1971. The stage hit *Fiddler on the Roof* came to the screen under Norman Jewison's direction, with Topol in the lead role of Tevye. The musical won Best Cinematography, Best Music, and Best Sound.

1972. Sally Bowles had been a striking character ever since Christopher Isherwood wrote about her. But she found her greatest glory in *Cabaret*—the Fred Ebb/John Kander musical brought to the screen with such flair by Bob Fosse. Liza Minnelli was Sally—and always will be.

1972. Not everyone was persuaded by Diana Ross as the great jazz singer Billy Holiday, but *Lady Sings the Blues*, directed by Sidney J. Furie, was an important step forward in telling black stories. Ross is shown in a scene with Billy Dee Williams, who played Holiday's lover, the gambler Louis McKay. The film also had a vivid supporting performance from comedian Richard Pryor.

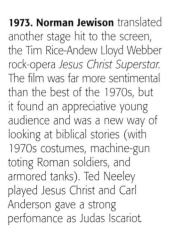

1973. Norman Jewison translated another stage hit to the screen, the Tim Rice-Andew Lloyd Webber rock-opera *Jesus Christ Superstar*. The film was far more sentimental than the best of the 1970s, but it found an appreciative young audience and was a new way of looking at biblical stories (with 1970s costumes, machine-gun toting Roman soldiers, and armored tanks). Ted Neeley played Jesus Christ and Carl Anderson gave a strong perfomance as Judas Iscariot.

1970s

1971. One of the sexiest women on screen in the 1970s was nearly eighty; Ruth Gordon and Bud Cort in Hal Ashby's *Harold and Maude*, one of the more unexpected and endearing hits of the time.

1973. It was inspired, if unlikely casting: Barbra Streisand as the Jewish radical and Robert Redford as Mr. America in *The Way We Were*. Arthur Laurents did the script, Sydney Pollack directed, Barbra sang the title song (by Marvin Hamlisch)—and there are still people crying out for a sequel.

1973. For years now, Glenda Jackson has been a Member of Parliament in Britain. But in the 1970s, she won the best actress Oscar twice—in *Women in Love* (1969), and here in *A Touch of Class*, with George Segal, directed by Melvin Frank.

1973. *Badlands* was based on the real case of Charles Starkweather, but as directed by Terrence Malick it made one of the greatest of American movie debuts—surreal, idyllic, horrific, a new kind of Western. It starred Martin Sheen and Sissy Spacek as the young runaways.

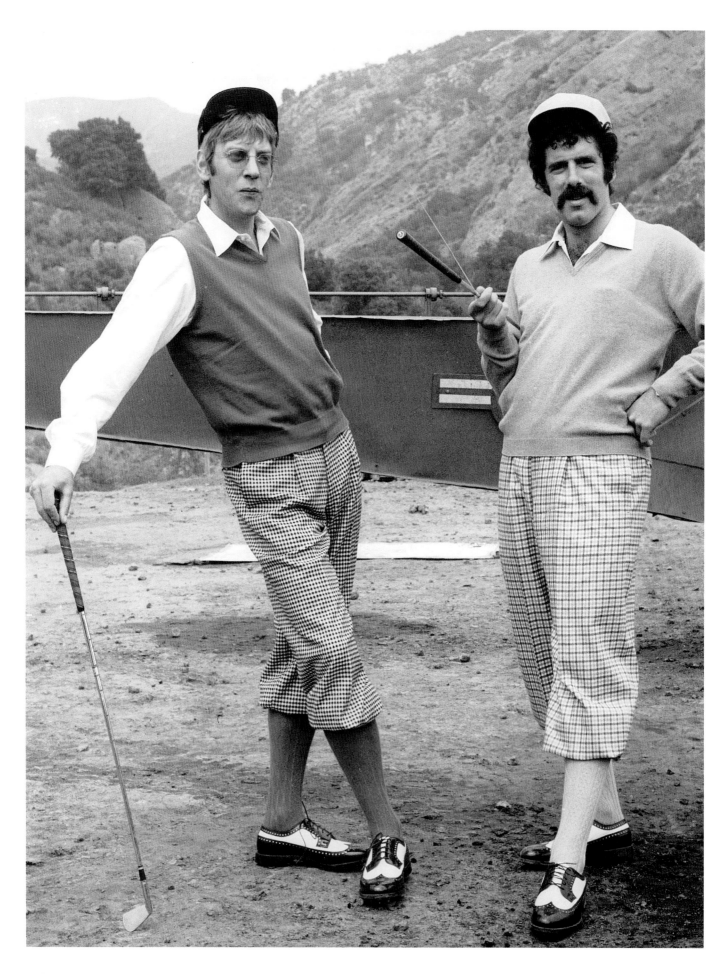

438

1970. Robert Altman would be a key director of the 1970s, and he signaled his arrival with the satire of *M.A.S.H.*, from a screenplay by Ring Lardner Jr. Donald Sutherland and Elliott Gould *(left)* played the two surgeons making light of the Korean war, team spirit, and so many other sacred cows.

1971. *With McCabe and Mrs. Miller,* Altman made a kind of anti-Western, druggy in mood, and propelled by the Leonard Cohen songs. It's a film that is revered more now than in its day, but it was always rooted in the fascinating tragicomic bond between Julie Christie and Warren Beatty *(right)*.

1973. Altman's dismantling of genres continued in *The Long Goodbye*, a brilliant modernist updating of the Raymond Chandler story. Elliott Gould was the new Philip Marlowe, and Nina Van Pallandt was one of the people who take him for a ride *(left)*.

1975. Altman's most ambitious picture was *Nashville*, a panorama of middle-America in which most of the actors wrote and sang Country and Western songs. In this scene, Ronee Blakley and Henry Gibson are at an open-air performance that will end badly *(left)*.

1977. According to Altman, *3 Women* began as a dream—and no one has ever been comfortable explaining all of its meanings. Still, it is one of his most beautiful movies, and it created a strange sisterhood between Shelley Duvall and Sissy Spacek. *(right)*. Janice Rule was the third woman, by the way.

1978. *A Wedding* was generally considered to be minor Altman. But it gives us the opportunity to show the meeting of Lillian Gish with the daughter of another great pioneer, Geraldine Chaplin *(left)*.

1972. There had been Mafia films since at least *Scarface* (1932). Writer-director Francis Ford Coppola was considered untried. No one was sure how to cast the film, or whether to trust the role of Vito Corleone to Marlon Brando. But in the end those two men stood by each other in *The Godfather*. In this on-set photo Brando and Coppola confer together on a scene *(right)*.

1972. A key moment in *The Godfather:* Michael (Al Pacino), the good brother, kills to defend the family honor *(left)*. The audience were by then completely on his side, and part of the power of *The Godfather* was to make us all eager to be Corleones.

1972. Brando as Vito, the old man, moments before the one natural death in the film *(right)*. Brando won his second Oscar for the performance and he helped inspire the cast of actors who had grown up in his tradition—Pacino, James Caan, Robert Duvall, and John Cazale.

1974. *The Godfather* **won** Best Picture and made a fortune—a sequel was certain. But it may be Coppola's greatest achievement that *The Godfather: Part II* is even better and a deepening of American history. Here is Robert De Niro as Vito the young man in that film. De Niro won Best Supporting Actor in the role, following Brando's Oscar for Best Actor—the only time two actors have won Oscars for playing the same character.

1974. The first two *Godfather* pictures are filled with fascinating supporting characters, and here are two of them from Part II— Robert Duvall as Tom Hagen, Michael's trusted lawyer or consigliere, and Michael V. Gazzo as mobster Frankie Pentangeli.

1974. In Part II, Michael's chief enemy is Hyman Roth (based on gangster Meyer Lansky). The role was taken by Lee Strasberg, who had been Al Pacino's teacher at the Actors' Studio.

1974. While he made *The Godfather: Part II*, Coppola also directed *The Conversation*, a story about sound, bugging and paranoia, enormously enriched by the performance of Gene Hackman and the sound design of Walter Murch.

1974. Increasingly, movies were made about movies—as takeoffs, as camp even. Mel Brooks made that approach a form of comedy, notably in the parody Western, *Blazing Saddles*, which starred Gene Wilder and Cleavon Little.

1974. Brooks turned to horror in *Young Frankenstein*. Gene Wilder had the lead role again, and the cast also included the fine comediennes Teri Garr and Madeline Kahn (who had been nominated for *Paper Moon*, and only lost to Tatum O'Neal), as well as Cloris Leachman (not shown here).

1975. *The Rocky Horror Picture Show* was more than parody. As a vehicle for audience participation, it became a late-night cult classic in college towns across the nation. Shown here are Tim Curry, Barry Bostwick, and Susan Sarandon.

1978. *Halloween* **had a simple idea** and a regular play date. The series began, under John Carpenter, as a story of menace in a small town, reliant on the guts of Jamie Lee Curtis.

447

1970s

1971. Steven Spielberg was twenty-three when he made *Duel*, and he had been making films for years. *Duel*, about a lone driver and a monster truck on the open highway, was made for television, with Dennis Weaver as the man. But it so impressed people that it began to play in theatres.

1974. *The Sugarland Express*, Spielberg's second film, was another kind of road film, in which a desperate mother (Goldie Hawn) hijacks a police car and its driver. Some people said it was just a routine melodrama, but some saw the kid had amazing skill.

1975. *Jaws* changed everything. With just a rubber shark and a cast that included Robert Shaw, Roy Scheider, and Richard Dreyfuss, Spielberg created a sensation that changed the film business. The movie taught all the kids on the beach that it might be safer, or more fun, at the movies. *Jaws* opened wide and created the big opening that dominates film marketing still.

1977. Steven Spielberg during the making of *Close Encounters of the Third Kind*. It was now clear that Spielberg was on his way to reenergizing the cinema of sheer wonder, and in the process identifying the vital teenage audience that might see a film over and over again.

1979. *Alien,* directed by Ridley Scott, launched a fascinating series about a mining spaceship attacked by an unstoppable, slimy creature stowed away onboard, and it introduced a great monster, designed by H. R. Giger *(left).*

1979. Sigourney Weaver's character Ripley was the last survivor of the space crew in *Alien (above)*—and then she realizes she is not alone. There is one more battle to fight (actually three, as in three sequels).

1970s

1973. A man who has been frozen for 200 years comes back to life: Diane Keaton and Woody Allen team together (in their first pairing) to save the planet in the futuristic comedy *Sleeper.* At this stage, Allen was still developing sight jokes and slapstick situations. But as time passed, his humor became increasingly verbal and psychological.

1975. No director worked more steadily than Woody Allen. With Diane Keaton as his frequent costar, Allen became a fixture in the 1970s with films like *Love and Death*.

1977. *Annie Hall* **was the first** climax of Allen's career, winning Oscars for Best Picture and Best Director as well as the prize for screenplay (to Allen and Marshall Brickman), and Best Actress for Keaton. It was also, notably, the first film in which Woody ventured to California.

1979. In general, New York was a vital part of Woody Allen's material, and in *Manhattan*—in black and white and with George Gershwin on the sound track—he made a love letter to the city.

1975. Another great New York movie was Sidney Lumet's *Dog Day Afternoon*, based on a real bank robbery. Al Pacino gave one of his best performances, as animated as Michael Corleone had been still *(left)*.

1976. At last, the movies launched a hilarious attack on television. *Network* starred Faye Dunaway *(right)*, Peter Finch, and William Holden and it was directed by Sidney Lumet. But the drive came from a Paddy Chayefsky script (once the prize TV writer in America) that launched the cry, "I'm as mad as hell, and I'm not going to take it anymore!"

1973. In *Serpico*, Sidney Lumet explored what would be his great theme: corruption within the police force of a large city. Al Pacino *(left)* played the undercover cop who finds conspiracy and nearly loses his life.

1975. It was more paranoia in *Three Days of the Condor,* when a CIA station gets wiped out. The lone survivor (Robert Redford) teams up with Faye Dunaway *(above).* Sydney Pollack directed and caught the prevalent mood of mistrust of government.

1975. Arthur Penn made the mystery movie, *Night Moves,* a study in paranoia where the intrigue is beyond the detective. In this scene, the detective (Gene Hackman) meets one of the most provocative teens of the 1970s—played by a very young Melanie Griffith *(left).*

1975. Written by Robert Towne and directed by Hal Ashby, *Shampoo* boosted the sexual reputation of Warren Beatty, who plays a Los Angeles hairdresser who seems in touch with every woman in the city. Here he is with Julie Christie *(right).*

1970s

1978. The influence of Hitchcock was common, and *The Eyes of Laura Mars* takes voyeurism and photography as its subject matter (like *Rear Window*). John Carpenter wrote it, Irvin Kershner directed. And Faye Dunaway starred with Tommy Lee Jones.

1976. *Rocky* was a phenomenon and a fairy tale in which an unsuccessful actor, Sylvester Stallone, wrote and starred in a fable about a boxer *(left)*. It won Best Picture and Best Director; it bred sequels and launched a career that is not over yet.

1976. Brian De Palma was a director with a big following, all of whom jumped time and again in the hysterical melodrama of *Carrie*—but never more so than at its shock ending. It was a story of high-school loneliness and sexual awakening, with Sissy Spacek in the lead role *(right)*.

1974. Martin Scorsese was the most emblematic new director of the age: he was crazy about movies; he was small and fragile, yet he had these intense dreams of violent street life. *Mean Streets* (1973) made his name, and then *Alice Doesn't Live Here Anymore*—with Ellen Burstyn winning an Oscar—proved his versatility.

1976. But Scorsese's *Taxi Driver* was the real sensation. Written by Paul Schrader, and starring Robert De Niro and Jodie Foster (as well as Cybill Shepherd and Harvey Keitel), it mixed in political disenchantment—the legacy of Vietnam—with the strange vigilante-killer Travis Bickle. Plus amazing violence. One of the most influential films ever made in America. Foster (who plays the child prostitute Bickle tries to save), De Niro, and Scorsese rehearse a scene.

1976. There were scenes in *Taxi Driver* made to display De Niro, talking to himself, to the camera, to us. Scorsese's rapport with De Niro would become central to his work. Thus, the actor who had played the young Brando in *The Godfather Part II* now took up Brando's legacy.

1977. Scorsese also loved musicals and—for a time—Liza Minnelli. All came together, with De Niro—in *New York, New York*, still one of his most remarkable and underrated pictures.

1970s

1974. Dustin Hoffman was one more great actor of the time. For director Bob Fosse, Hoffman did an inspired job of impersonation as the outrageous political comedian, Lenny Bruce in the film, *Lenny*.

1976. In Alan J. Pakula's *All the President's Men* (with a brilliant Oscar-winning screenplay by William Goldman) Hoffman and Robert Redford played Carl Bernstein and Bob Woodward, the two journalists at *The Washington Post* who did so much to uncover the Watergate intrigue. Jason Robards won a supporting actor Oscar for his role as executive editor Ben Bradlee.

1976. Hoffman's many pictures included *Marathon Man* (directed by John Schlesinger), in which Laurence Olivier was the worst advertisement for dentistry anyone had ever dreamed of.

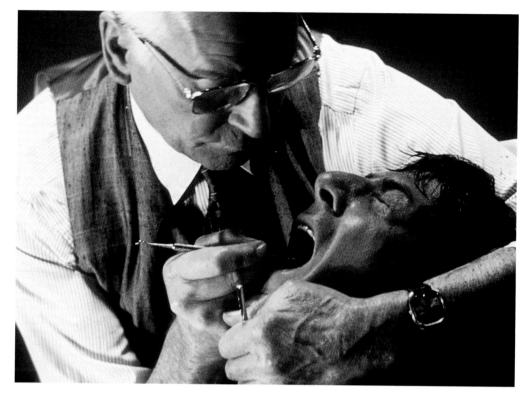

1979. It was in the divorce drama *Kramer vs. Kramer* that Hoffman won his Oscar. Robert Benton directed and the role of the wife was taken by a newcomer who would become a great figure in American film, Meryl Streep.

1973. *American Graffiti* was George Lucas's memory of growing up in a small Californian town, dreaming of cars, music, sex, and getting away. The exuberant young cast included Candy Clark and Charlie Martin Smith, seen here with Ron Howard *(above)*. The film also starred Richard Dreyfuss, and in a small role, Harrison Ford.

1977. This is George Lucas with Alec Guinness on location for *Star Wars*. Lucas was a kid from Modesto, California, shy and quiet, who became part of the Coppola gang in San Francisco. In time, he would surpass Coppola in terms of material success and business influence.

1977. Twentieth Century Fox
financed *Star Wars*, but they
were very insecure about the
film, and whether the odd mix of
science fiction and comic books
would find an audience. It turned
out to be the most influential
film of the late twentieth century,
the crystallization of the chemistry
between young viewers and
special effects. In a classic scene
from the film, the Force steers
Peter Mayhew, Mark Hamill, Alec
Guinness, and Harrison Ford.

1977. It was in the creation of
special effects and computer-
generated imagery—all based at his
offshoot, Industrial Light and Magic,
in San Rafael, California—that Lucas
was most creative and dominant
(as evidenced in this space-
battle scene from *Star Wars*).
Nearly twenty-five years later, the
full saga is not yet finished.

1970s

1975. Herb Ross's *The Sunshine Boys (right)* came from a Neil Simon play about the reunion of two veteran vaudeville performers. The comedy owed everything to the performances of Walter Matthau and George Burns (who won Best Supporting Actor).

1978. During the late 1970s, in feature films and concert pictures, Richard Pryor became increasingly popular. Pryor played with Bill Cosby *(left)* in one of the episodes in *California Suite*—four stories, set at the Beverly Hills Hotel, written by Neil Simon and directed by Herbert Ross.

1977. Neil Simon's name was everywhere. *The Goodbye Girl*, also directed by Ross, was an adaptation of one of his plays. It concerned a young actor and a divorcee who have to share an apartment. Marsha Mason starred with Richard Dreyfuss, who won the Oscar for Best Actor *(right)*.

1977. Shut out of the room in *The Godfather*, and only a sidekick in the Woody Allen films, Diane Keaton found a big role as the sexually adventurous woman in Richard Brooks's *Looking for Mr. Goodbar*. It was candid and alarming, and one of many films with a new interest in women. Keaton is working here with newcomer Richard Gere *(right)*.

1978. *Heaven Can Wait*, codirected by Warren Beatty and Buck Henry, was a remake of *Here Comes Mr. Jordan* (1941). Beatty played the football player who is allowed to come back to Earth after death—and meets Julie Christie *(left)*.

1978. French Director Louis Malle made *Pretty Baby*, about a whore and her daughter, and their relationships with a photographer (Keith Carradine). Susan Sarandon and Brooke Shields *(right)* played the lead roles and Sven Nykvist was responsible for the luminous photography.

1978. Vietnam was back with a vengeance in *The Deer Hunter*, an extraordinary epic which switched suddenly from an American steel town to the Vietnam jungle. Some said it was politically and historically dishonest. But no one could deny the emotional force of Michael Cimino's film and the cast that included Christopher Walken, John Savage, John Cazale, Meryl Streep and (seen here, *left*) Robert De Niro.

1978. Written by Oliver Stone, with a tense score by Giorgio Moroder, *Midnight Express* was one of the best films about drugs. Directed by Alan Parker, it starred Brad Davis as the young American who falls foul of the law in Turkey *(right)*.

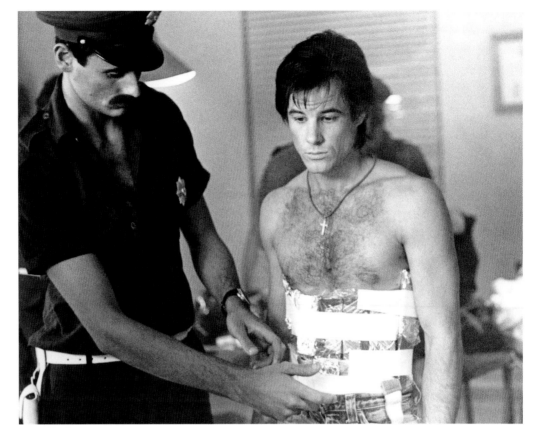

1979. Very few American films have ever dealt with trade unionism. But Martin Ritt's *Norma Rae* was the glowing exception, and it won Sally Field an Oscar playing the woman who organizes a textile factory in North Carolina *(left)*.

1979. *10* **was a hit comedy** of the late 1970s, written and directed by Blake Edwards, with Bo Derek as the perfect nymph and Dudley Moore as the restless man *(left)*. The film made Derek a sex symbol, inspiring legions of women to braid their hair.

1979. *Being There* was adapted by Jerzy Kosinski from his own story. It concerned a humble gardener—a simpleton even— whose cryptic remarks seem so full of wisdom that he becomes an advisor to the president. Hal Ashby directed and Peter Sellers caught the mysterious air of the gardener *(right)*.

1978. Newcomer Christopher Reeve was the perfect, clean-cut actor to play the comic book hero, *Superman*, directed by Richard Donner *(left)*. The film also starred Margot Kidder as Lois Lane and Gene Hackman as the evil Lex Luthor.

1977. John Travolta had played in *Welcome Back, Kotter* on TV and acted in a few films. All of a sudden, disco made him a star in *Saturday Night Fever*, where he and Karen Lynn Gorney were a winning dance team. John Badham directed, and the music came from the Bee Gees.

1978. Travolta was a natural for the male lead in *Grease*, Randal Kleiser's smash-hit movie of the stage hit. Olivia Newton-John played the female lead and kids everywhere went crazy for the 1950s pastiche.

1978. The big reason for seeing and admiring *The Buddy Holly Story* was Gary Busey's performance as the rock singer who died so young. Busey did a lot of his own singing.

1979. *All That Jazz* was the story of Bob Fosse and his reckless battle with heart disease—directed by Fosse himself. In this scene, we see Ben Vereen with Roy Scheider who played Fosse and danced the exacting routines.

1979. *Hair* **was as big** a flop on screen as it had been a hit on stage, despite the wit of Milos Forman's direction and the stylish choreography by Twyla Tharp *(left)*.

1979. Plenty of people felt that Bette Midler wasn't exactly Janis Joplin. Still, *The Rose (above)*, directed by Mark Rydell, was one of those films that caught the passions of a rock-and-roll career, with outstanding concert scenes.

1970s

1979. In Francis Ford Coppola's Vietnam War epic *Apocalypse Now,* Martin Sheen played Willard, the young officer who is sent up a jungle river to terminate the renegade Green Beret Kurtz's command. Along the way he meets the air cavalry and their Colonel Kilgore, played with panache by Robert Duvall *(right).*

1979. Filmed in the Philippines in mounting chaos, *Apocalypse Now* came from a John Milius script (with commentary by Michael Herr), and it was a version of Joseph Conrad's *Heart of Darkness.* It reunited Francis Ford Coppola with Marlon Brando, who played Colonel Kurtz *(left).*

1979. Martin Sheen in the dreamlike conclusion to *Apocalypse Now (right),* photographed by Vittorio Storaro (he won Best Cinematography). The controversial film divided critics but drew large audiences. It was 2001 before Coppola released a longer version that was hailed as a masterpiece.

1980s

1983. Lawrence Kasdan's *The Big Chill* was a portrait of the thirty-something generation, raised in the 1960s, but mellowed by age, sadness, and the new materialism. It was an ensemble film, based on the death and burial of one of the group—a part given to Kevin Costner, and then cut. So the film is famous for Kevin Kline, Jeff Goldblum, Glenn Close, Tom Berenger, Wiliam Hurt, JoBeth Williams, and Mary Kay Place *(right)*.

1980. *Raging Bull* was for many people the American film of the 1980s. Martin Scorsese's story of boxer Jake LaMotta was sordid in subject matter, yet ecstatic in treatment. Art and violence were held in balance by the director's vision and the mesmerizing performance by Robert De Niro *(left)*, who won his Oscar for Best Actor. *Raging Bull* was also a testament to black-and-white photography.

1988. *Die Hard* *(previous pages)* was typical of the dynamic yet fanciful action franchises that prevailed in the 1980s. Bruce Willis was the ordinary cop who could handle all manner of mayhem (invariably delivered by suave English villains). There have been three in the series so far, and for a while their noisy success tended to mask Willis's cool subtlety as an actor.

1980s

The Space Operas Begin

In the 1980s, the movies and television were joined by video-cassettes, cable TV, and something called the Internet. Many argued that as the entertainment business spread (with increasing corporate control), so the quality of movies declined. In response, the phenomenon of "independent" film developed: projects funded cheaply outside the system for more discerning (and smaller) audiences. That flux has not ended yet, and it has been complicated by the fascination with special effects and their startling ways of satisfying the old dream—to see things we have never seen before. Thus *The Terminator*, *Aliens*, the *Star Trek* series and even *Who Framed Roger Rabbit*.

George Lucas and Steven Spielberg became more dominant figures—often in partnership (as on the *Indiana Jones* pictures). Lucas took the *Star Wars* story through several sequels, and Spielberg stretched his wings with *E.T.*, *The Color Purple*, and *Empire of the Sun*.

There were also ambitious and more realistic ventures like *Reds*, *Atlantic City*, *Tootsie*, *The Right Stuff*, *Amadeus*, *Out of Africa*, and *Driving Miss Daisy*; one of several movies that displayed a new sophistication over race. Some great directors died—Alfred Hitchcock, William Wyler, John Huston (but not before *Prizzi's Honor*), and Vincente Minnelli. But there were newcomers, too, like Oliver Stone, Spike Lee, Jonathan Demme, and David Lynch, whose *Blue Velvet* suggested that the art picture and the mainstream could overlap.

There were fresh faces: Harrison Ford; Michael Douglas (*Fatal Attraction* was a sensational event); Robin Williams; Arnold Schwarzenegger; Tom Hanks; Tom Cruise; Meryl Streep; Susan Sarandon; Jessica Lange; Sally Field; Sigourney Weaver; Morgan Freeman; Nicolas Cage.

1980. *The Elephant Man* had the same theme as *Raging Bull* (beauty and the beast), yet was very different in period and place. Derived from the stage play about the real life of nineteenth-century Englishman John Merrick, it was directed by the experimental filmmaker, David Lynch, and produced by none other than Mel Brooks (who originally hid his name from the credits because he felt he was too closely associated with comedy). John Hurt won admiration for his work as Merrick, and he was supported by Anthony Hopkins as his doctor.

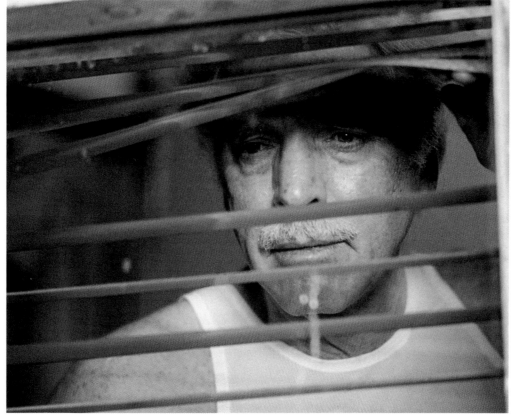

1980. *Atlantic City* was filmed in a place seldom used in American movies, and its theme was novel, too: that of a veteran dreamer who had always wanted to behave like someone in a movie, and who gets his chance. From a fine script by John Guare, and directed by Louis Malle, it cast Burt Lancaster, and helped illuminate his great career. In this scene, he is watching Susan Sarandon bathing after coming home from work in an oyster bar.

1980. What is Jack looking at in the end of *The Shining*? It's Jack Torrance or Jack Nicholson, the caretaker at the Overlook Hotel who finds his lost identity there—to the detriment of his family. Stanley Kubrick recreated the Colorado hotel in England, yet this was an emphatically American film, drawn from Stephen King, in its mix of horror, family problems, and screwball comedy.

1980. On *The Shining* set with cameraman John Alcott, Kubrick lines up a shot in the Overlook bar—the place where Jack Torrance will dream up the perfect, if sinister, barman (played by Kubrick regular Joe Turkel).

1981. David Mamet did the script for Bob Rafelson's remake of *The Postman Always Rings Twice,* and the picture achieved a burning, poisonous relationship between Jack Nicholson and Jessica Lange.

1985. *From a Richard Condon novel,* and in the leisurely hands of John Huston, *Prizzi's Honor* is maybe the best of Mafia comedies. Jack Nicholson was superb as a slow-on-the-uptake made man. Kathleen Turner was his dangerous sweetie. And Anjelica Huston was waiting to pounce.

1980. Richard Gere in the poster image for Paul Schrader's *American Gigolo*—a role once set for John Travolta. Again, the subject (male prostitution) was offset by the stylishness of the approach. Designed by Ferdinando Scarfiotti, it was a film fascinated by male fashion, décor and lighting, the gay aura, and the new Los Angeles (plus disco).

1982. Richard Gere and Debra Winger may not have got on too well together, but they worked on screen in Taylor Hackford's *An Officer and a Gentleman*, which combined romance, military training, rebelliousness, and unexpected views of working-class life.

1980s

1980. The most awaited picture of the year was the continuation of the *Star Wars* story. In *The Empire Strikes Back* (directed by Irvin Kershner), the originals met the mystic Yoda *(right)*. The special effects were better than ever, and the box office response was the more striking for being overlooked at the Oscars. George Lucas had changed the movies—but it would be eleven years before the system gave him the Irving Thalberg award.

1980. By now, it was clear that the saga had a great, ambiguous villain—Darth Vader (played by David Prowse, *left*, but spoken by James Earl Jones). Such figures became household items in the toys and games that helped make George Lucas the wealthiest man in the picture business.

1983. *Return of the Jedi* was another great *Star Wars* hit, with Mark Hamill and Carrie Fisher *(right)*, whose own hectic Hollywood career would later produce the book and film *Postcards from the Edge*.

1980. ***Coal Miner's Daughter*** was part of the growing interest in celebrities and show-business figures. Written by Tom Rickman and directed by Michael Apted, it was the story of country singer Loretta Lynn. Sissy Spacek *(right)* played the lead and won the Oscar—and she did a lot of her own singing in the film.

1980. ***Urban Cowboy*** came from a magazine article about a lifestyle type: the urban Texan who likes to act like a cowboy. John Travolta played the lead and his partner was the lively newcomer Debra Winger *(left)*, who had a spectacular scene riding a mechanical bull.

1980. All over the world, women were concerned about their role and their position in life. One comic exploitation of that interest had the ageless Goldie Hawn in the Army as *Private Benjamin (right)*—directed by Howard Zieff. Over twenty years later, with a daughter acting, Ms. Hawn could still play the part!

1980. The dysfunctional family was a new concern, and Robert Redford made his directing debut with *Ordinary People* (from the Judith Guest novel), in which Timothy Hutton played the son of Mary Tyler Moore and Donald Sutherland. In this scene, he's with his psychiatrist, Judd Hirsch. Redford and Hutton won Oscars and *Ordinary People* took Best Picture.

1981. *Arthur wasn't* just dysfunctional—he was a wreck. He was also the subject of a comedy written and directed by newcomer Steve Gordon. It was a throwback to screwball in which Dudley Moore finds true love, at last, with Liza Minnelli. But he needed the help of his valet (John Gielgud, who won the supporting actor Oscar). Gordon's high promise was cut short by his death in 1982.

1981. *On Golden Pond* was a fond tribute to veterans. Jane Fonda was behind the picture (directed by Mark Rydell) and the casting of her father and Katharine Hepburn. Henry Fonda died next year. Hepburn won her fourth Oscar but would make only a few more films.

1981. The new cynicism about movie stars centered on *Mommie Dearest*—the exposé book by Joan Crawford's adopted daughter Christina, which became a movie directed by Frank Perry. Faye Dunaway was brilliant as Crawford, but in the process the real actress was buried in camp mockery.

1980s

1981. In the first year of Ronald Reagan's presidency, who would have expected Hollywood's most respectful tribute to American Communists? *Reds* was the story of John Reed, and the dramatization was intercut with interviews of real witnesses from history. Warren Beatty played Reed and directed—and he won the directing Oscar.

1981. Based on fact, with a script by Jay Presson Allen and director Sidney Lumet, *Prince of the City* was an enquiry into corruption in the New York City police force and a study in bureaucratic stealth. It starred Treat Williams, seen here with Richard Foronjy.

1981. Directed by Sydney Pollack, *Absence of Malice* was an intriguing story of ethics in the newspaper business. It paired Paul Newman, as an innocent but ambivalent man, and Sally Field as the reporter on his trail.

1982. *Tootsie* **was a long time** in the making, with many screenwriters trying to sort out the problems. Yet it seemed like an inspired comedy made on a perfect afternoon. Sydney Pollack directed and Dustin Hoffman played a small-time actor who dresses up as a woman to keep in work, becoming a famous soap opera star. Hoffman falls in love with his costar on the soap, Jessica Lange, who won Best Supporting Actress.

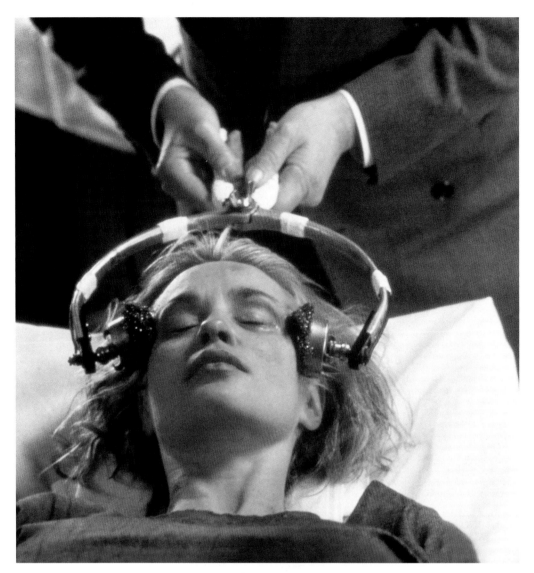

1982. Frances Farmer was a brilliant, beautiful actress of the 1930s—but she made trouble. And she ended up in an asylum, suffering electroshock therapy and a lobotomy. *Frances* (directed by Graeme Clifford) was not easy watching, but it showed that King Kong's girlfriend, Jessica Lange, had grown into a great actress (after winning the supporting Oscar for *Tootsie* she was also nominated for *Frances,* in the same year).

1982. It was a time for rare actresses: Meryl Streep won the Oscar for *Sophie's Choice,* adapted from the William Styron novel and directed by Alan J. Pakula. Streep, playing a Holocaust survivor, is seen here in a happier moment, with Kevin Kline and Peter MacNicol. The gentle color imagery was by cinematographer Néstor Almendros.

1982. Barry Levinson was from Baltimore, and for his directing debut he made *Diner*, a small film about kids growing up in that city. The result was funny, touching and a big hit. Levinson was set as a director, and he helped bring in a wave of young actors—sitting around the table, *from left to right:* Kevin Bacon, Mickey Rourke, Steve Guttenberg, and Daniel Stern.

1982. She was Nastassia Kinski then (she would be Nastassja later) and one of the most haunting new faces. Paul Schrader cast her as the young woman whose fears and hopes are fulfilled in *Cat People*—an erotic remake of the 1942 horror movie that expressed the dichotomy of the human subconscious.

1980s

1982. In a wintry Boston, an alcoholic lawyer gets his last chance at redemption in a negligence suit against a big hospital. David Mamet wrote the script for *The Verdict* and Sidney Lumet directed. Paul Newman gave what many regard as his finest performance as the lawyer. James Mason was his opponent in court.

1983. Larry McMurtry's novel *Terms of Endearment* was the directing debut of James L. Brooks, and good enough to win Best Picture and Best Director. It was a story of generations: the kids were Jeff Daniels and Debra Winger. But here we see the elders—Shirley MacLaine and Jack Nicholson—rediscovering love.

1987. If you've seen the inside of a television station, you know the definition of crazy humor. *Broadcast News* exploited that theme and entertained everyone. Writer-director James L. Brooks was already a titan of TV, but he worked with his stars—Albert Brooks, Holly Hunt, and William Hurt—to make one screen work for another.

1986. Beth Henley's play, *Crimes of the Heart,* was like Chekhov's *The Three Sisters* set in the South. Bruce Beresford directed, and the women were Diane Keaton, Jessica Lange, and *(left)* Sissy Spacek.

1980s

1982. Based on the Philip K. Dick story, *Do Androids Dream of Electric Sheep?*, *Blade Runner* was a very influential sci-fi film for both its vision of a future city and its feeling for the plight of androids. The movie's setting—a dark, moody, crowded L.A. in 2019—set the standard for urban sci-fi design. Director Ridley Scott is seen here working with Harrison Ford *(right)*, on his way to being the biggest box-office actor of the 1980s.

1982. Ford's character was the "blade runner" of the title, a cop as bounty hunter, sent out to terminate renegade "replicants," or androids. Rutger Hauer *(below)* was memorable as the haunting and dangerous android, Batty—a top of the line "combat model."

1982. Steven Spielberg produced *Poltergeist,* about a family under siege in their own home. Directed by Tobe Hooper, this was horror for real—and all the more startling in that the television set was the spirits' point of contact with their lives. In this still *(left)* Craig T. Nelson and JoBeth Williams try to figure out what their daughter (played by Heather O'Rourke) means when she says: "They're here . . ."

1982. *With E.T. the Extra Terrestrial,* Spielberg magically fused science fiction and the dreams of young children—but the result appealed to audiences of all ages. There are few images in American film as simple, profound, and fantasy-laden as E.T. saying good-bye to Elliot, played by Henry Thomas *(below). E.T.* became the biggest box-office film to that date.

501

1982. In Disney's *Tron,* Hacker Jeff Bridges is abducted into the world of a computer and forced to fight in gladiatorial games—he can only escape with the help of a program Tron, personified by Bruce Boxleitner (seen here with Cindy Morgan, *right*). The film was visionary for its time, both for its computer-generated effects and its portrayal of what it might be like in cyberspace, before the word even existed.

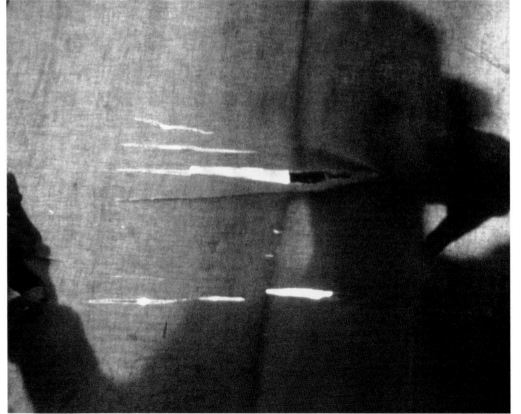

1984. *A Nightmare on Elm Street* was Wes Craven's first film in a series about a demonic figure, Freddy Krueger (Robert Englund, *left*) who could enter the minds of teenagers and murder them through their dreams.

1986. *Aliens*—the continuing adventures of Sigourney Weaver's Ripley—proved to be an extraordinary battle movie, thanks to the drive of director James Cameron. For all that violence, it was clear that Weaver herself was urging more tenderness into the story, and just as Ripley was a heroine she was a surrogate mother to Carrie Henn (*right*).

1984. Take a smart-ass Detroit cop; make him black; cast Eddie Murphy; and dump him down in Beverly Hills. It wasn't quite that simple. Martin Brest directed and Murphy was at his peak as a public attraction in *Beverly Hills Cop (left)*.

1982. *48 Hrs.* was the *Odd Couple* as cops—Nick Nolte needs Eddie Murphy to help him find a very bad guy *(right)*. Walter Hill directed what proved to be a very influential form of comedy and action, and the welcome novelty of a black man and a white man learning to get along.

1987. *Lethal Weapon* was the start of another bonanza franchise in which you could see the outlines of *48 Hrs*. Richard Donner directed, and Danny Glover and Mel Gibson were the ill-assorted cops who have to work together *(left)*.

1980s

1982. Peter Weir's *The Year of Living Dangerously* was a love story set in Indonesia in the time of President Sukarno. There was a rare sense of place, weather, and fear, and great chemistry between Mel Gibson and Sigourney Weaver, as an Australian journalist and a British diplomat.

1983. So many remakes are disappointing. But Brian De Palma's *Scarface* is a match for the Howard Hawks film made fifty years earlier. The inspiration in the script (by a beginner named Oliver Stone) was to have the hero as a Cuban who lands in Miami. It's violent, funny, and very American, and Al Pacino's Tony Montana is one of his greatest roles—still imitated by kids all over the country.

1983. In the years since *Apocalypse Now*, Francis Coppola had suffered decline and near bankruptcy at the time of *One from the Heart* (1982). He made a comeback in 1983 with two films from Susie Hinton books: *The Outsiders* and *Rumble Fish*, both starring Matt Dillon. Young hood Dillon talks to his older brother (Mickey Rourke) in a scene from *Rumble Fish*.

1984. No one had heard of Joel and Ethan Coen until *Blood Simple* opened at the New York Film Festival—and then everyone wanted them. Joel directed, Ethan produced, and they shared the writing. As for their star, Frances McDormand, there was no sharing—Joel would marry her.

1980s

1983. Most people rejoiced when that outstanding supporting actor, Robert Duvall, found a starring part—a washed-up country singer in Bruce Beresford's *Tender Mercies (right)*. Duvall sang, and went off with the Oscar.

1983. Karen Silkwood was a real woman who lived, and died, working at an Oklahoma nuclear factory. Nora Ephron and Alice Arlen turned it into a script called *Silkwood*. Mike Nichols directed. And Meryl Streep found the rough, funny, redneck troublemaker in her acting soul *(far right)*.

1983. In the 1980s, movie advertising (in print and on TV) was more crucial than ever. This is from a knockout poster for *Risky Business (left),* the breakthrough film for Tom Cruise and a celebration of Rebecca De Mornay.

1983. She's a welder by day and a sexy dancer at night. Yes, it's a crazy fantasy, but *Flashdance* was a movie—or a music-video movie—that proved a sensation. Jennifer Beals was the woman *(left),* Adrian Lyne directed, and a dark star called Joe Eszterhas was one of the screenwriters.

1985. Teenagers were in: they were the audience and the subject matter, and no one told their story better than John Hughes. Redhead Molly Ringwald was on the cover of *Time* to epitomize the moment. In *The Breakfast Club (right),* she endured a memorable day of detention with, *from left to right:* Ally Sheedy, Judd Nelson, Anthony Michael Hall, and Emilio Estevez.

1980s

1986. _Top Gun_ and the jet aircraft were the best vehicles Tom Cruise had found yet _(left)_. Macho in every way, the film made Cruise a superstar. Tony Scott directed.

1987. Open to so much, Steven Spielberg next turned to J. G. Ballard's vivid autobiographical novel about growing up in Shanghai and being a prisoner of the Japanese. _Empire of the Sun_ was scripted by Tom Stoppard and it starred Christian Bale as the boy _(below)_. For some viewers it is one of Spielberg's most impressive movies.

1983. Philip Kaufman's _The Right Stuff_ was adapted from Tom Wolfe's book about the first U.S. astronauts. But it went one better than Wolfe in that the aviation heroics were combined with a satire on America and its media. Here we see Sam Shepard as Chuck Yeager _(right)_, the greatest of America's test pilots.

1980s

1984. *Places in the Heart* was set in Texas during the Depression, and it was written and directed by Robert Benton (who had worked the same territory in *Bonnie and Clyde*). But this was a simpler study of poverty and race. This still shows Danny Glover and Sally Field, who would win her second Oscar for the film. Yes, that's when she cried out that "I can't deny the fact that you like me . . . right now . . . you like me!"

1984. *The Cotton Club* had been a great nightclub in Harlem in the 1930s—with black acts and white audiences, and gangsters all over the place. Francis Ford Coppola took on the subject, hiring William Kennedy to do the dialogue. It was full of music and a romantic story that involved Richard Gere and Diane Lane.

1985. Little Lukas Haas is *Witness* to a murder. That's how the Philadelphia underworld and a cop (Harrison Ford) found themselves in Amish country. The contrast was very dramatic, and Peter Weir turned the thriller into a love story and a reflection on violence.

1985. *The Color Purple* was a novel by Alice Walker, an emotional epic on black life in the South. Steven Spielberg took it on, with a cast that included Whoopi Goldberg as the heroine, Celie; and Margaret Avery and Oprah Winfrey as the two women who help her. There were mixed feelings about the result, but no one could question the extraordinary range and industry of Spielberg. Here, Akosua Busia (Nettie) and Desreta Jackson (young Celie) share a joyful moment as sisters playing in the field.

1981. E. L. Doctorow's great novel *Ragtime* was brought to the screen by Milos Forman. The part of the police chief was a fond farewell for James Cagney, so often a terror to the cops.

1983. It was always clear that Barbra Streisand intended to do more than sing and act. In *Yentl*, she did those things, and directed too. Here she is working with costars Mandy Patinkin and Amy Irving in the story taken from Isaac Bashevis Singer. It's a fine film, with gorgeous songs by Michel Legrand.

1984. Robert Towne wrote *Greystoke: The Legend of Tarzan, Lord of the Apes* as more than a Tarzan sequel. He was fascinated by ape behavior. But he had to give up the project to director Hugh Hudson. French actor Christopher Lambert played Lord Greystoke, seen here with the man who discovered him, Captaine Phillippe D'Arnot (Ian Holm).

1986. Written by Robert Bolt (who had done *A Man for All Seasons*), Roland Joffé's *The Mission* was a story of church and state in the colonial history of Latin America. Robert De Niro was the converted slave trader and and Jeremy Irons played the man of God.

1984. *Amadeus* was nominated for eleven Oscars and it won eight—yet Mozart didn't get a nod. It came from the play by Peter Shaffer, about the strange relationship of Mozart and Salieri. Milos Forman commanded all the diverse elements and won glorious performances from Tom Hulce as the genius and F. Murray Abraham as the hack. Emperor Joseph (Jeffrey Jones) looks on (*left*) as Mozart plays.

1988. Christopher Hampton had done a play from the epistolary novel (it's all letters) by Laclos. Then Stephen Frears gave it screen immediacy, with Glenn Close and John Malkovich made for each other as the wicked, conspiring sensualists who plot Michelle Pfeiffer's downfall in *Dangerous Liaisons* (*above*).

1984. Ron Howard's delightful comedy, *Splash*, concerned the love affair between a mermaid (looking as good as Daryl Hannah above the scales) and Tom Hanks (who didn't yet quite resemble America's everyman on the screen).

1984. *Swing Shift* involved women going to work in factories during the Second World War. Jonathan Demme directed, even if there were arguments with his star and producer, Goldie Hawn—seen here with Kurt Russell, who would become her companion in life.

1984. Carl Reiner's *All of Me* was an ingenious comedy about the spirit of Lily Tomlin invading the body of Steve Martin. It was also a sign of how frequently television comedians were now shifting over to the big screen.

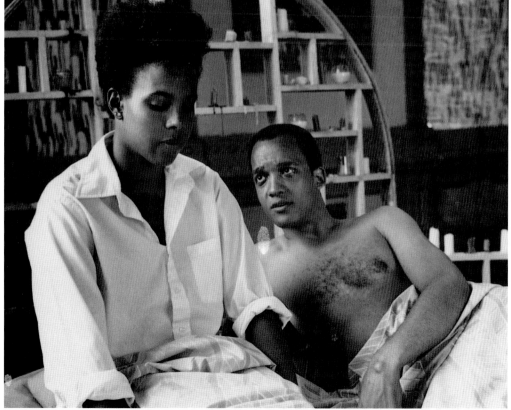

1986. Spike Lee was a young director who made a striking debut with *She's Gotta Have It,* starring Tracy Camilla Johns and Tommy Redmond Hicks. The movie was made on nerve and credit cards, and it was emblematic of Lee's lasting audacity.

521

1984. James Cameron was little known, until he cowrote (with Gale Anne Hurd) and directed *The Terminator*. It was a very cunning story in which the end became the beginning. It had state-of-the-art special effects. But above all, it found the perfect part for Arnold Schwarzenegger, the Austrian bodybuilder who was about to become an icon.

1984. Indiana Jones was the accumulation of all the cinema's adventure heroes. He made his debut in the smash hit *Raiders of the Lost Ark* (1981), and the franchise developed momentum with *Indiana Jones and the Temple of Doom (right)*. Steven Spielberg directed, and George Lucas wrote. Harrison Ford was Indy and untouchable.

1984. You can't beat silly, simple ideas—like four guys who do what *The Exorcist* did with more laughs. Call for *Ghostbusters*, written by Dan Aykroyd and Harold Ramis and directed by Ivan Reitman. The four musketeers were Ernie Hudson, Bill Murray, Aykroyd, and Ramis.

1985. Bob Gale and Robert Zemeckis came up with the idea for *Back to the Future*—and there were three films in the series, all directed by Zemeckis. It was a cute idea, but it worked so well because of the affectionate interaction of Michael J. Fox and Christopher Lloyd. Steven Spielberg produced—he was everywhere; and nearly every time he had a hit.

1980s

1984. Woody Allen still worked more steadily than anyone. The quality varied, but in the 1980s he ran into a rich period, starting with *Broadway Danny Rose*, which gave Mia Farrow a wonderful opportunity as a gangster's moll.

1985. *The Purple Rose of Cairo* was one of Allen's best films. Its subject was nothing less than the fantasy interaction of people on the screen and those in the audience. The ensemble cast was headed by Jeff Daniels and Mia Farrow.

1986. *Hannah and Her Sisters* was vintage Woody Allen, in a Chekhovian mood. Mia Farrow, Barbara Hershey, and Dianne Wiest were the sisters and the cast also included Michael Caine (who won his first supporting Oscar—so did Wiest). As ever, New York was the background and a big part of the subject.

1987. If Jim Brooks could make a film about TV, Woody Allen hit on radio. *Radio Days* is a wondrous panorama of the 1930s, a gallery of small stories and incidents—with Woody's narration and a medley of hit songs. Here we see Allen directing Mia Farrow.

1980s

1984. John Carpenter's *Starman* was a true love story for sci-fi fans. Jeff Bridges played the lost alien and Karen Allen was the woman who helps him—and has to deal with the way he looks like her late husband.

1985. Could you believe that nice Jeff Bridges would murder anyone—with a *Jagged Edge*? His lawyer, Glenn Close, couldn't, but she's falling in love with him. All we'll say is that Joe Eszterhas wrote the film and betrayal is his big subject. Richard Marquand directed.

1988. Francis Coppola's fondness for innovative and thwarted inventors flowered in *Tucker: The Man and His Dream*, the story of a real-life artist in the automobile business. Jeff Bridges did his customary good work in the lead.

1989. For sheer pleasure it was hard to surpass *The Fabulous Baker Boys,* in which Michelle Pfeiffer played a torch singer who comes between Jeff and Beau Bridges. Newcomer Steven Kloves directed and Pfeiffer sang her own songs.

1980s

1985. In *Out of Africa*, Meryl Streep gave yet another astonishing performance as the Danish writer, Karen Blixen. Sydney Pollack directed what was a love story (Robert Redford played the English hunter), a tribute to Africa and flight, and a study of a writer finding herself.

1986. The difference between an actress pretending to be deaf and an actress with true hearing loss shines through in this moment from *Children of a Lesser God*, where Marlee Matlin feels the dance music. Randa Haines directed. William Hurt was the costar. And Ms. Matlin won the Oscar.

1985. The veteran actress Geraldine Page (she died in 1987) won the Oscar in Peter Masterson's adaptation of Horton Foote's play, *The Trip to Bountiful*, about an old lady going home for a last look. She is seen here with Rebecca De Mornay.

1986. *Blue Velvet* came out of nowhere. It was a Dino de Laurentiis production, and the most lucid fairy tale David Lynch has ever managed: a portrait of the psycho-sexual ordeal in coming of age. It starred Kyle MacLachlan, Isabella Rossellini, *left,* and Dennis Hopper, and it was one of the most controversial films of the decade.

1984. Haing S. Ngor, a former doctor who escaped from the Khmer Rouge in 1979, won the supporting actor Oscar in Roland Joffé's film *The Killing Fields,* a tragic panorama of Cambodia's recent history. Sam Waterson played the journalist who befriends him *(above).*

1986. Oliver Stone's breakthrough, and a new attitude to combat in Vietnam, coincided in *Platoon,* where the soul of a few soldiers is determined by the moral conflict between two sergeants (played by Tom Berenger and Willem Dafoe—seen here with Mark Moses, *right). Platoon* won Best Picture and Best Director.

1987. Still working in England, Stanley Kubrick made *Full Metal Jacket,* a film about basic training and real combat in a ruined Vietnamese city. In this scene *(left),* a wounded Arliss Howard is rescued.

1989. In Oliver Stone's obsessive reexamination of recent American history, *Born on the Fourth of July* threw a harsh spotlight on Vietnam again. It was the story of paralyzed vet Ron Kovic, played by Tom Cruise *(below).*

1987. *Street Smart,* directed by Jerry Schatzberg, had Christopher Reeve as a New York magazine writer looking for a hot subject—and finding more than he bargained for. It was notable for drawing attention to two supporting players: Kathy Baker and Morgan Freeman (seen here with Reeve).

1987. *The Untouchables* came from the old TV series, and it was Al Capone vs. Eliot Ness. But Brian De Palma gave it an extra cinematic edge, and hinged the story on the relationship between Ness (Kevin Costner) and the last honest cop in Chicago (Sean Connery—who won the supporting actor Oscar). In this photo they are flanked by Charles Martin Smith and Andy Garcia.

1988. The murder of some civil rights workers in Mississippi in 1964 is the provocation for *Mississippi Burning,* in which Gene Hackman and Willem Dafoe are FBI agents investigating the case. Englishman Alan Parker directed. The cinematography, by Peter Biziou, won an Oscar.

1988. *Rainman,* **the story** of an idiot savant and his selfish, materialist brother, proved difficult during the script stage. But Barry Levinson stepped in and pulled the project together—thanks to outstanding work from Dustin Hoffman and Tom Cruise. Hoffman won his second Oscar, but people were just as impressed with Cruise.

1986. In *Something Wild* *(right)*, a very straight guy gets swept off his feet and into danger by a girl who has different names and hair styles—all of which belong to Melanie Griffith. Jeff Daniels was superb as the guy, and Jonathan Demme let the high spirits turn very dark as soon as Ray Liotta appeared in the story.

1986. Sex was generally less pressing a subject than it had been in the last age of censorship, but *Nine 1/2 Weeks* was—quite simply—an erotic exercise, much influenced by director Adrian Lyne's training in commercials and the unquestionable carnal appeal of Kim Basinger and Mickey Rourke *(left)*.

1987. *The Witches of Eastwick* was an extravagant comedy, directed with flourish by George Miller and adapted from the John Updike novel. The New England devil was a perfect meal for Jack Nicholson and his lovely conquests were Cher, Susan Sarandon, and Michelle Pfeiffer *(right)*.

1980s

1987. *Fatal Attraction* was the talking point of the year. There were arguments over the ending and on how true to life it was. But the adulterous affair in which the other woman suddenly becomes deadly serious gripped everyone. And under Adrian Lyne's direction, there was combustible chemistry between Glenn Close and Michael Douglas.

1987. Italian-Americans weary of Mafia attitudes glamorized on screen found some comfort in the delightful comedy, *Moonstruck*. John Patrick Shanley's script was well handled by Norman Jewison, and the romance between Nicolas Cage and Cher was a charming surprise. For Cher, it meant the Oscar.

1987. Time and again, good movies concerned the human urge to dance. *Dirty Dancing,* set in a resort hotel in the Catskills, drew athletic performances from Jennifer Gray and Patrick Swayze.

1988. *The Accidental Tourist* proved that an audience existed for careful adaptations of good novels. The source was Anne Tyler; the director was Lawrence Kasdan. The unusual character studies were played out by Kathleen Turner and (seen here), William Hurt and Geena Davis—she won the supporting actress Oscar.

1980s

1984. Bernard Malamud's mystical novel about baseball, The *Natural*, was filmed by Barry Levinson with Robert Redford perfect casting as golden boy Roy Hobbs (*right*).

1989. Does Kevin Costner love baseball? Three times so far. But *Field of Dreams* (directed by Phil Alden Robinson) was the real hit and surprise. It's the story of an ordinary guy who builds a field—and waits for them to come. Costner is seen here with Burt Lancaster and Gaby Hoffman (*left*).

1988. Ron Shelton had served his time as a baseball player before turning to the movies as writer and director. Thus, his *Bull Durham* stands as one of the most authentic sports movies— it had Kevin Costner and Tim Robbins as players, and Susan Sarandon as the groupie who really appreciates their stats (*right*).

1988. *It was a measure* of the extra understanding Dian Fossey had given us about gorillas that in many scenes Sigourney Weaver could work with the real animals *(left)*. At the same time, under Michael Apted's direction, *Gorillas in the Mist* revealed just how confused and confusing a person Fossey had been.

1988. Based on a real case, *The Accused* had an Oscar-winning performance from Jodie Foster as a rape victim. Kelly Mcgillis played her lawyer and Jonathan Kaplan directed. The strength of Foster's performance (and her character's case) depends on the full, foul-mouthed provocation of the wronged woman. This still shows Foster and Mcgillis besieged by reporters outside the courtroom *(right)*.

1988. For years Martin Scorsese had wanted to do a realistic life of Christ (stressing the ordinary man), inspired by the Nikos Kazantzakis book. It came to life as *The Last temptation of Christ* with Willem Dafoe as jesus *(left)*. The religious right tried to have the film banned. Their protests actually sent more people to see it—proving the first law of censorship.

541

1980s

1987. As everyone made his or her bundle (and box office numbers appeared in every newspaper) Oliver Stone caught the craze for profit in *Wall Street*, with the idea "greed is good." Who better to offer that perilous motto than Michael Douglas—on his way to an Oscar.

1988. Sylvester Stallone had two macho series going in harness. The *Rocky* films went on through the decade in increasingly fanciful boxing matches. But when Sly wanted to get in shape he did a Rambo—this is *Rambo III* (behind the lines in Afghanistan—not that the lines mattered in these films).

1989. *Drugstore Cowboy* was a small, independent picture, made by Gus Van Sant. But few films had caught the moods and talk of drugs so well, or been less moralizing. Matt Dillon, as the leader of a crew that robs pharmacies, is seen here in a not-too-friendly embrace with a small-time dealer, played by Max Perlich.

1989. Spielberg again with another smash hit: *Indiana Jones and the Last Crusade*. But, if Harrison Ford wasn't enough— and he was, throughout the decade—this time Spielberg gave him a father, played by Sean Connery. No one guessed it then, but it was the last Indy film we've had.

1988. After *Pee-wee's Big Adventure*, Tim Burton really arrived with *Beetlejuice*, a film that expressed his astonishing visual imagination and his absorption in comic books. Michael Keaton played the wild spirit who gooses up the lives of ordinary souls *(left)*.

1988. Even more startling was the seamless mix of live action and animated characters in *Who Framed Roger Rabbit*—which was also director Robert Zemeckis's answer to *Chinatown*. Bob Hoskins played the private eye, seen here with Jessica Rabbit *(right)*—who had a voice by Kathleen Turner and songs by Amy Irving, but was drawn as a very naughty toon.

1989. Tim Burton hit it very big with *Batman*, a dark variation on the Bob Kane comic character, and a film dominated by Jack Nicholson's show as the Joker *(left)*. People remarked on how much Jack earned in profits from the huge hit. But he knew that that's what stars do.

1980s

1989. *Crimes and Misdemeanors* was one of Woody Allen's more serious films. It turned on the way one character (Martin Landau) has an inconvenient woman (Anjelica Huston) murdered—which reunites him with his criminal brother (Jerry Orbach, who nearly always represents law and order). Landau and Orbach plot here in a scene from the film.

1989. No one had heard of Steven Soderbergh, but his debut, *Sex, Lies, and Videotape* (which really was a movie about little more than talking heads), won the Palme d'Or at Cannes and Soderbergh was on his way. This scene involves Andie MacDowell and James Spader.

1989. Everyone laments the death of education, but no one does anything. Then along came Peter Weir with *Dead Poets Society*, written by Tom Schulman and dedicated to the hope of great teachers—and ambitious students. Robin Williams played the teacher.

1989. *Steel Magnolias,* directed by Herbert Ross, was a nice movie about the women who go to a beauty parlor in a small southern town. It had a large, excellent cast, but people with the right instincts said "that's the one to watch"—it's Julia Roberts, dancing with Tom Skerritt.

1986. Rob Reiner's *Stand by Me* is one of the best films ever made about American childhood. Adapted from Stephen King and narrated by Richard Dreyfuss, its young cast included Corey Feldman, River Phoenix, and Wil Wheaton.

1988. *Big* **was a knockout comedy** with a five-word idea: a kid becomes grown up. Tom Hanks was the twelve-year-old who wakes up thirty, and it was clear that his natural energy and good nature were perfect for the joke. So was director Penny Marshall. Hanks and Robert Loggia try out the keyboard at FAO Schwartz.

1988. *Working Girl* was a skilled romantic comedy suggesting that anyone with natural smarts and creative thinking can make it to the top in business — providing her unethical boss was conveniently out of the office, laid up with a broken leg. It was directed by Mike Nichols, with Harrison Ford as an investment banker torn between Melanie Griffith (the working girl with a "head for business and a bod for sin") and Sigourney Weaver (the boss).

1989. It's the scene that made delis desirable again. Nora Ephron did the script; Rob Reiner directed; and it's Meg Ryan faking the orgasm while Billy Crystal fakes calm in *When Harry Met Sally*. We'll have what she's having.

1980s

1989. You can't beat history.
Glory was the story of the first black regiment raised by the Union during the Civil War. Edward Zwick directed and Matthew Broderick was the white officer but the film was a gallery for great black actors: Denzel Washington, Morgan Freeman, Andre Braugher, and many others *(right)*.

1989. Spike Lee came of age with the magnificent interracial observation of *Do the Right Thing*, a study of heat, noise, and general aggravation in a city that resembled New York. Lee is seen here with Richard Edson *(left)*.

1989. A gentler but maybe even more effective story of race was *Driving Miss Daisy*, directed by Bruce Beresford from the play by Alfred Uhry. It starred Jessica Tandy and Morgan Freeman *(right)* and won the last Best Picture Oscar of the decade.

1990s

1990s

The Cinema Goes Electronic

More than ever, Hollywood in the 1990s felt like a business aimed at the 15–24 age range. All the studios now belonged to worldwide media giants (Sony, Viacom, Rupert Murdoch's News Corporation, AOL Time Warner, and Vivendi). So many movies (like the *Scream* pictures) were spoofs of older conventions. Instead of being stories for which we suspended disbelief, some movies now were camp parodies through which kids mocked the medium itself.

The rapid development of special effects shifted movies from being photographed narrative to electronic events that could never exist. And sometimes it was hard to remember that movies had begun as the dreamlike duplication of real life.

That aspect of the 1990s is told in the *Batman* franchise (begun in 1989), *Terminator 2*, the realization of the age of dinosaurs in *Jurassic Park*, *Independence Day*, and *The Matrix*. At the same time, James Cameron's *Titanic* mixed effects with an old-fashioned love story and redefined the level of box-office expectations. So expensive to create, that epic was damned in advance, only to become the most successful film ever made. *Titanic* had Leonardo

DiCaprio, too, and the age remained susceptible to new young faces—Tom Cruise, Julia Roberts, Brad Pitt, Johnny Depp, Gwyneth Paltrow, Jennifer Lopez. But the decade also witnessed a number of uniquely ambitious pictures that took on large subjects and renewed the tradition of classic entertainment: *Dances with Wolves*, *The Silence of the Lambs*, *Unforgiven*, *Forrest Gump*, *Schindler's List*, *Pulp Fiction*, *Shakespeare in Love*, and *The Sixth Sense*.

Meanwhile, *The Blair Witch Project* gave warning that with just a camcorder and the Internet, it was possible to fashion a sensation.

1990. The face of the year
belonged to Julia Roberts, one of
the liveliest stars of the 1990s.
With its roots in prostitution,
Pretty Woman (right) was a sign
of how far Disney had grown up.
It was also an adroit turning of its
own set-up in the direction of a
classic Cinderella story. Garry
Marshall directed. Richard Gere
was the perfect male model as
the rich man. But Julia was the
magical element.

1990. If anything persuaded
Warren Beatty to get married,
it may have been trying to keep
up with Madonna. Their (brief)
partnership in real life was
repeated on screen in Beatty's
very pretty, very expensive
comic-book movie, *Dick
Tracy (left).*

1990. There were more films
about death being transcended
(the ultimate American dream?).
So in *Ghost (right)*, death did
not entirely divide Demi Moore
and Patrick Swayze. Seeing dead
people (or people who were
more and less than real) would
be a theme of the age.

1990. The new child millionaire of the movies was Macaulay Culkin *(right)*, the star of *Home Alone* and its sequels. The violent comedy was all from the boy's point of view. Chris Columbus directed the original, in which Master Culkin meted out rough justice to Daniel Stern, Joe Pesci, and anyone else who got in his way. Hardly anyone asked, "Why is the kid alone?"

1990. Martin Scorsese reckoned that *The Godfather* films were artistocratic. So he set out to show the ordinary lower-class Mafia life in *Goodfellas*. Along the way, he made one of the most vivid films about drug paranoia. Here, Ray Liotta shows Robert De Niro and Joe Pesci what's in the Balducci's bag.

1990. Pulp novelist Jim Thompson (who had written for Kubrick in the 1950s) was attracting Hollywood attention. Stephen Frears took on *The Grifters*, which had fine performances from John Cusack and Annette Bening. But Anjelica Huston *(right)* was the standout as a mother who has her own son as a rival in the con game.

1991. Warren Beatty loaned his intriguing mixture of shyness and flamboyance to Ben Siegel, aka Bugsy *(left)*, the man who built the first great casino in Las Vegas and who died because he was a better dreamer than businessman. Beatty starred with his wife-to-be, Annette Bening, in a picture written by James Toback and directed by Barry Levinson.

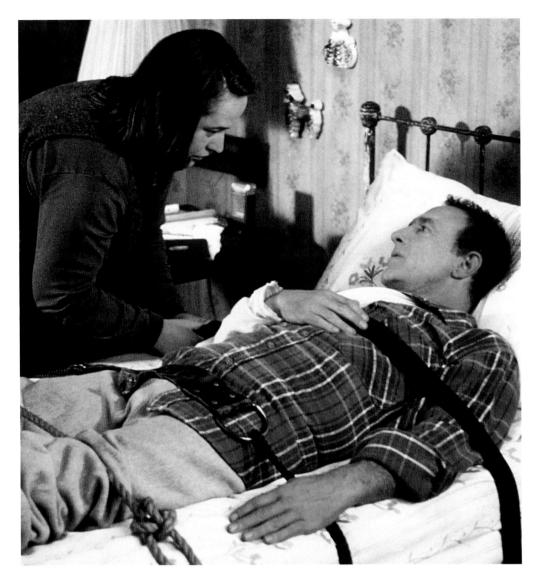

1990. One of the best versions of the artist-meets-mad-fan story is Stephen King's *Misery*. The versatile Rob Reiner did a full-blooded version with James Caan as the injured novelist and Kathy Bates as the smothering nurse (she won an Oscar). It was part of a vengeful, black mood directed at celebrities on and off screen.

1991. With a good script by Callie Khouri, *Thelma & Louise* was that rarity, a female buddies-on-the-road movie. Ridley Scott gave it intense visual energy, especially as it reached the American southwest, and as the man who had directed Sigourney Weaver's Ripley in *Alien,* he won terrific performances from Susan Sarandon and Geena Davis.

1991. *My Own Private Idaho*
wasn't Hollywood, but it was one
of those independent films that
made the country pay attention.
In part this was because of
Gus Van Sant's direction, but it
was also a tribute to the cast that
included Keanu Reeves and
River Phoenix (seen here), who
would be dead two years later.

1991. Martin Scorsese did a
remake of *Cape Fear,* in which
Robert De Niro played the old
Robert Mitchum role with a scary
sense of evil. There was a nasty
edge to the picture but it had
fine performances from Nick Nolte
(being choked here, by De Niro),
Jessica Lange, and Juliette Lewis.

1990s

1991. The look of the year. He admitted the role was quite easy—and it wasn't very long. But anyone who saw *The Silence of the Lambs* came away imitating like Anthony Hopkins's Hannibal Lecter *(right)*. Novelist Thomas Harris's villain had entered folklore—and, strangely, we loved him. It won Best Picture, Best Director (Jonathan Demme), Best Actor, and Actress (Jodie Foster).

1991. *Terminator 2: Judgment Day* was one of those films where artificial life fought with the real thing—thanks to spectacular special effects. Arnold Schwarzenegger made a neat side step from villain to hero, Linda Hamilton repeated her gutsy heroine, and James Cameron made sure that the suspense never flagged. In this still Robert Patrick's deadly cyborg—or what's left of him—takes aim at the heroes *(left)*.

1991. Talking of ghosts, *The Addams Family* at last arrived on the big screen. Former cameraman Barry Sonnenfeld judged the black humor nicely and he was blessed with the creepiest functioning family ever—Judith Malina, Christina Ricci, Raul Julia, Carel Struycken, Anjelica Huston, Christopher Lloyd, and Jimmy Workman *(right)*.

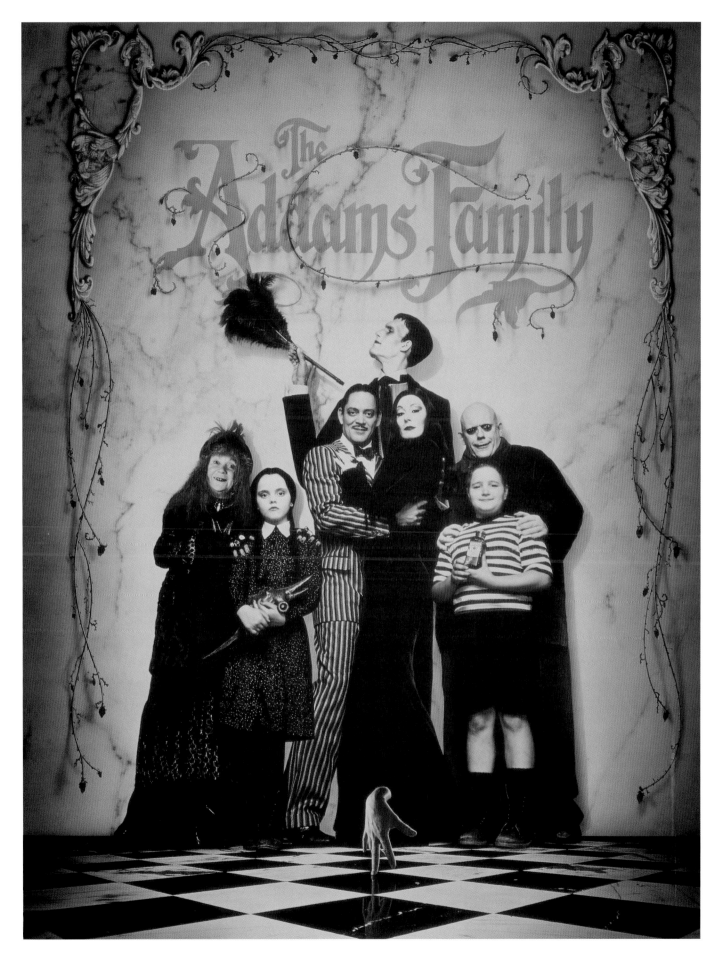

1992. Al Pacino had never won an Oscar. The prize came—as is sometimes the case—in something less than his best work. *Scent of a Woman* had him as a blind, depressed ex-military officer. He was delightful. The film was hokey. And the tango lesson he gave Gabrielle Anwar was the memorable scene *(left)*.

1992 Brad Pitt and Craig Sheffer take instruction from director Robert Redford on location for *A River Runs Through It (right)*, taken from Norman Maclean's autobiographical novella—maybe the best film about fly-fishing (and the first?) ever made in Hollywood.

1992. Clint Eastwood was still a star, but the 1980s had been his quietest time. He came back with *Unforgiven*, a Western that shattered many illusions about heroism. The rich cast included Morgan Freeman, Richard Harris, and Gene Hackman, who won the supporting actor Oscar. The film won for Best Picture and Best Director for Clint *(left)*.

1990. The surprise of the year was Kevin Costner's directorial debut. *Dances with Wolves (above)* had a feeling for the Sioux nation that no Hollywood film had known. It was an epic in length and ambition, yet told so simply and powerfully that Costner carried off Best Picture and Best Director. In later pictures (like *Waterworld* and *The Postman*), Costner's simplicity looked a little naïve. But he is an authentic storyteller.

1991. The most controversial film of the year (and many years) was Oliver Stone's *JFK*—which was rather as if Barton Fink had written the Warren Report. Kevin Costner played New Orleans D.A. Jim Garrison *(right)* in a movie more in love with film than history maybe, but absolutely unforgettable.

1992. Long ago, *The Bodyguard* had been a Lawrence Kasdan script intended for Steve McQueen. But in Mick Jackson's version it was a vehicle for Kevin Costner and Whitney Houston—as such it was one of the rare interracial love stories in American film *(left)*.

1995. Kevin Costner played the Mariner in the amazing *Waterworld (below)*. Why "amazing"? Because the idea was so audacious, but not quite as perilous as the cost of production. So the picture became famous as a folly as Follywood tried to persuade itself that it would be economy-minded.

1992. It took a hundred years before anyone thought of a title as good and universal as *Basic Instinct*—but screenwriter Joe Eszterhas dreamed it up. Paul Verhoeven directed one of the sexiest films of the decade, thanks to the willing and often unclothed efforts of Sharon Stone *(left)* as the psychopathic seductress and Michael Douglas as her willing prey.

1992. It was still Michael Keaton as the masked man in *Batman Returns* (directed by Tim Burton), but most eyes were on Michelle Pfeiffer's delicious, neurotic Cat Woman *(right)*—the most beguiling screen feline since *Bell, Book, and Candle*.

1993. Adrian Lyne's *Indecent Proposal (left)* was pretty silly: Robert Redford pays $1 million for a night with Demi Moore (everyone knew her price for a movie was far higher). But the melodrama of sex and money appealed to the current mood.

1994. The new comic talent of the age was Jim Carrey. He followed *Ace Ventura: Pet Detective* with *The Mask*, directed by Charles Russell. Carrey is a bank clerk who is transformed into a zany superhero after finding a magic mask, stealing the heart of Cameron Diaz *(left)*. His career would build with *Dumb and Dumber*, *Batman Forever*, and *The Cable Guy*.

1994. Disney's *The Lion King* *(right)* was a significant step forward in the animated movie in that much of its humor and storyline was more for adults than children. The songs were by Elton John and Tim Rice; the outstanding voice cast included Matthew Broderick (Simba), Jeremy Irons (Scar), Nathan Lane (Timon), and Whoopi Goldberg (Shenzi).

1995. *Toy Story* *(left)* was distributed by Disney, but it was the work of John Lasseter and the Pixar studio. The animation was computer-generated, but the toy characters were made endearing with the voices of Tom Hanks (Sheriff Woody), Tim Allen (Buzz Lightyear), and Don Rickles (Mr. Potato Head).

1991. With *Barton Fink*, the Coen Brothers delivered an inspired, surrealist fantasy about life in Hollywood in the alleged golden age. John Turturro was the playwright who goes West and then farther out.

1991. The ever-ingenious Albert Brooks delivered one of his most personal films with *Defending Your Life (right).* Brooks plays a fearful (dead) ad executive who ends up in Judgment City, where he must prove in court that he lived courageously before he can move on to the next level. (Meryl Streep was a fellow defendant who was Prince Valiant in one of her previous lives). It was somehow vital to the self-deflating comedy of Brooks that chance had assigned him to the age of Woody Allen. Without Woody, Albert would be known as a genius.

1992. With a script by Michael Tolkin, Robert Altman bounced back into prominence with *The Player*, a clever, sardonic satire on Hollywood life-styles. The large starry cast revolved around a studio boss played with relish by Tim Robbins.

1992. Fannie Flagg's novel about female friendship in the South turned into *Fried Green Tomatoes*, directed by Jon Avnet. The two leads were Jessica Tandy and Kathy Bates. It was a sign of how far women's lives had become acceptable in a medium generally dominated by male fantasies.

1992. Spike Lee's most ambitious picture yet was the biographical epic *Malcolm X*, a film of many moods and styles, bound together by the superb performance of Denzel Washington.

1992. There were several problems with Richard Attenborough's *Chaplin* (including the narrative structure), but Robert Downey Jr. was a marvel as the comic himself. Downey's path has not been smooth, but he is one of the most mercurial actors in America.

1993. With Tina Turner delivering the songs, Angela Bassett gave a high-voltage performance in *What's Love Got To Do With It*. This was a biopic on Ike and Tina Turner (Laurence Fishburne played Ike) directed by Brian Gibson.

1997. The marked increase in the Hispanic population within the United States has led to a new sense of Latina stars, as witness the career of Jennifer Lopez, launched in the biopic *Selena*, directed by Gregory Nava.

1991. *Boyz N the Hood* was a potent survey of black life in South Central Los Angeles, and further proof of the scope for black vision in American film. John Singleton directed and the cast included such future names as Cuba Gooding Jr. and Ice Cube *(left)*.

1992. Carl Franklin's *One False Move* began as a crime movie set in Los Angeles, but then shifted to Arkansas and became a study of race and family—one of the best small films of the decade. Its players included Cynda Williams and Billy Bob Thornton *(right)*, who also cowrote the script. He and Franklin would have significant careers ahead.

1992. Quentin Tarantino was a film-mad kid who worked in a video store. He knew it all. And then he got the chance to do it—first of all in *Reservoir Dogs*, very violent, very funny, very formal, all at the same time. The guys on parade *(left)* are Michael Madsen, Tarantino himself, Harvey Keitel, Chris Penn, Lawrence Tierney, Tim Roth, and Steve Buscemi.

1991. Pat Conroy's very popular if rather old-fashioned novel, *The Prince of Tides*, was ideal material for the polished sentiments and enquiring psychology of Barbra Streisand. She acted in the film, too, and coaxed a brilliant performance from Nick Nolte.

1992. Michael Mann had already made striking films like *Thief* and *Manhunter* (actually the screen debut of the Hannibal Lecter character). But he established himself with the stunning *The Last of the Mohicans*, in which Daniel Day-Lewis played Fenimore Cooper's hero, Hawkeye.

1993. It was a big step to go from *Cape Fear* to Edith Wharton's *The Age of Innocence*, but Martin Scorsese was eager for fresh fields. We see him here directing Winona Ryder and Daniel Day-Lewis.

1993. Amy Tan's best-selling novel, *The Joy Luck Club*, was brought to the screen by Wayne Wang (born in America to Chinese parents). It told stories about the old country and the new, and the tangled relationships of mothers and daughters. In this scene, we see Tsai Chin and Tamlyn Tomita.

1993. The great, self-appointed task that faced Steven Spielberg was *Schindler's List,* a film about the concentration camps and the strange providence of Oskar Schindler. Liam Neeson and Ben Kingsley were the two men who save Jews from death *(left).* The film won seven Oscars, including Best Picture and Best Director.

1993. Shot in luminous black and white (photography by Janusz Kaminski), the film was exceptional in making a Nazi a powerful character. This owed a lot to Ralph Fiennes's uncanny performance *(below, center).*

1993. *Schindler's List* was remarkable by any standards. Yet, at the same time, Spielberg also handled the special effects revolution of *Jurassic Park (right).* It was as if someone had been Beethoven and Irving Berlin in the same year.

1992. The film was called *Bram Stoker's Dracula,* and it was true to the original novel, but it sprang from the imagination of Francis Coppola and owed a lot to its Oscar-winning makeup, décor, and costumes. Gary Oldman was the vampire, with Winona Ryder as the object of his obsession *(left).*

1994. Few writers had a bigger following than Anne Rice, and her work reached the screen with Neil Jordan's *Interview with the Vampire.* Tom Cruise *(right)* was the debonair and malevolent Vampire Lestat. The cast also included Brad Pitt, Christian Slater, Antonio Banderas, and Kirsten Dunst.

1994. Still lusting after controversy, Oliver Stone made *Natural Born Killers* (from a story by Quentin Tarantino), a lurid satire on the media, sex, and violence. Woody Harrelson and Juliette Lewis *(left)* played the madcap killers on the road.

1993. It became a game that could span the globe, but *Six Degrees of Separation* was a John Guare play before Fred Schepisi turned it into a movie. The central socialite couple were played to perfection by Stockard Channing and Donald Sutherland.

1993. Working from several stories by Raymond Carver, Robert Altman's *Short Cuts* was a group portrait of people living in Los Angeles on the fault line. The amazing cast included Lili Taylor, Robert Downey Jr., Chris Penn, and Jennifer Jason Leigh.

1993. Lasse Hallström was an outstanding Swedish director who came to America to make *What's Eating Gilbert Grape*. It was another opportunity for Johnny Depp and Juliette Lewis, but they both gave way to the dazzling performance by a new kid named Leonardo DiCaprio.

1994. Paul Newman was seventy in 1995, but he contributed several dry old-timers to the decade—notably *Nobody's Fool*, directed by Robert Benton from Richard Russo's novel. In that film, as well as in *Twilight* and *Message in a Bottle*, Newman proved that the less he did the better he became.

1992. The real history of women's baseball during World War II was alluded to in Penny Marshall's *A League of Their Own* in which Tom Hanks was the drunk managing a team that included Rosie O'Donnell and Madonna (both seen here) as well as Geena Davis.

1993. *Sleepless in Seattle* was a very popular romantic comedy in which the lovers are strangers for much of the film. But fate and Nora Ephron's direction bring them together. They were Tom Hanks and Meg Ryan—endearingly ordinary people—and Ross Malinger played Hanks' son.

1993. *Groundhog Day* was a cunningly original comedy about a man trapped in a 24-hour loop. Directed and cowritten by Harold Ramis, it also made admirable use of the talent of Bill Murray (a funny man yet a real actor), pictured in a scene with Andie MacDowell.

1994. *True Lies* was a peculiar cross-breed. Like most Arnold Schwarzenegger films, it had a lot of action and explosions. But there was also a subtext—about men and women—that seemed to come from left field. James Cameron directed and Jamie Lee Curtis was Arnold's wife.

587

1993. Old television shows were coming back as big pictures: *The Fugitive* was directed by Andrew Davis. Harrison Ford was the man on the run and Tommy Lee Jones won the supporting actor Oscar as the cop chasing him.

1993. Director Sydney Pollack working with Tom Cruise on the set of *The Firm*. This was one of several pictures taken from John Grisham novels, and one of a larger group that played into our equal fear of and fascination with the law (a condition much heightened by the O. J. Simpson trial).

1993. In Wolfgang Petersen's *In the Line of Fire*, Clint Eastwood played a presidential security man who needs to vindicate himself. But his major problem is one of the more artful and chatty villains of the decade—fondly played by John Malkovich.

1994. A Los Angeles bus will explode if its speed drops below fifty miles an hour. That is what high concept means. So you call the picture *Speed*. You put Keanu Reeves on the bus, with Sandra Bullock. You hire in Dennis Hopper as the villain. Go! Jan De Bont directed and had a hit for his debut. In real life, of course, you won't find an L.A. bus that can do fifty!

1995. "Houston, we have a problem." And when you're in space, problems make better movies than smooth success. *Apollo 13* was the story of a moon mission that lived with potential disaster. Ron Howard directed and the three guys in the capsule were Kevin Bacon, Tom Hanks, and Bill Paxton *(left)*.

1992. *A Few Good Men* *(left)* was a gripping, old-fashioned courtroom drama, with the difference that it was a military court. Rob Reiner did another good directing job. Demi Moore was the female interest. But the picture focused on a stirring duel between Tom Cruise and Jack Nicholson.

1995. Cold War attitudes died hard, and Tony Scott's *Crimson Tide* was a conflict between hard-core military thinking and a new moderation, all set on a nuclear submarine but reminding us of the Bounty. The forces were personified by Gene Hackman and Denzel Washington *(right)*.

1994. Stephen King provided the source material for writer-director Frank Darabont's *The Shawshank Redemption*. It was a parable about prison and freedom, with beautiful performances from Morgan Freeman and Tim Robbins.

1995. David Fincher is the most stylish pessimist among Hollywood's new directors, and *Se7en* is his most striking work yet. It follows the efforts of two cops, Morgan Freeman and Brad Pitt, to track down an uncommonly erudite and intellectual serial killer. Not to ruin the suspense, but let's just say that Kevin Spacey also stars.

1995. In the 1990s, the death penalty was still at work in America. *Dead Man Walking* was a subtle and fair dramatization of the issue, all based on fact, with Sean Penn as the killer and Susan Sarandon as the nun who tries to help him. She won her Oscar and thanked the director, her companion in life, Tim Robbins.

1995. One of the most emotionally searing films of the decade was Mike Figgis's *Leaving Las Vegas*, the love story between an alcoholic and a Vegas hooker. Made very cheaply, it found a large audience thanks to the performances of Elisabeth Shue and Nicolas Cage (who won the Oscar).

1990s

1994. Tarantino's glory came at Cannes where *Pulp Fiction* won the Palme d'Or. It then went on to great box-office success. The serpentine structure involved several story-lines and a host of stars, but John Travolta and Samuel L. Jackson were the hit men who went through (and stole) the whole show *(right)*.

1995. Martin Scorsese did Las Vegas in *Casino*, a dazzling panorama of that dazzling place. It was another exercise for Scorsese's guys (notably Robert De Niro and Joe Pesci), but Sharon Stone delivered a gorgeous turn as the foul-mouthed, cocaine-raddled, and jewelry-fixated "Ginger" *(below)*.

1995. Just when you thought the impossibly twisted thriller was a thing of the past, along came *The Usual Suspects (left)*, written by Christopher McQuarrie and directed by Bryan Singer. Reading from *left to right,* the lineup is Kevin Pollak, Stephen Baldwin, Benicio Del Toro, Gabriel Byrne, and Kevin Spacey. So how do you spell Keyser Soze?

1997. Taken from the James Ellroy novel, Curtis Hanson's *L.A. Confidential* was remarkable for its period recreation, its love story, and its beautifully tricky plot. Australian Russell Crowe was a hit as one of the cops, and Kim Basinger won the supporting actress Oscar as a hooker in the Veronica Lake style.

1995. There were too many dumb films for teenagers, maybe, but there were smart ones, too. *Clueless*, written and directed by Amy Heckerling, was a high-school comedy inspired by Jane Austen's *Emma*. Alicia Silverstone (seen here with Stacey Dash) made a big impact in the lead.

1996. In the 1960s, Jerry Lewis had made his masterpiece with *The Nutty Professor*. Over thirty years later, and with a ton of special effects, Eddie Murphy had another hit with the same material—even if his movie was less comic and a lot less disturbing.

1997. Julia Roberts faltered in the mid-1990s, but she was back in form with *My Best Friend's Wedding* (written by Ronald Bass and directed by P. J. Hogan). In this still Julia gives a little speech for her two costars, Cameron Diaz and Dermot Mulroney.

1998. "Gross-out" became a term of critical praise with *There's Something About Mary*, directed by Bobby and Peter Farrelly. Evidently, the public's taste levels were being pushed in all directions—and the teenage audience was greedy for more. The leads were played by Ben Stiller and Cameron Diaz (demonstrating a new extra-hold hair gel).

1997. Gus Van Sant's *Good Will Hunting* was a tribute to education and emotional honesty, with Matt Damon as a brilliant but resistant student and Robin Williams as the psychologist who helps him. Oscars went to Williams and to Damon and his friend Ben Affleck for their screenplay.

1997. The director Ang Lee had done beautiful work with Taiwanese characters and stories. Then he pulled off Jane Austen's *Sense and Sensibility*. Next, he captured American life in the 1970s with *The Ice Storm*, a poignant study of parents and children, which starred Sigourney Weaver and Kevin Kline.

1997. Woody Allen had experienced bad press for personal reasons, but some fans believed his work was becoming ever more clever. *Deconstructing Harry* was about a writer who offends friends by putting them in his books. It was funny, yet very serious. Another all-star cast included a grown-up Mariel Hemingway, the wise child from *Manhattan*.

1997. Jack Nicholson was sixty and working a little less. But he seized the opportunity of the grouchy guy in *As Good As It Gets*, directed and cowritten by James L. Brooks. Both stars, Helen Hunt and Nicholson, won Oscars—her first, his third. With one more he matches Katharine Hepburn's record.

1996. "They" said the Michael Ondaatje novel, *The English Patient*, couldn't be filmed. But they did not factor in the skill of writer-director Anthony Minghella, a cast that included Ralph Fiennes and Kristin Scott Thomas, and the resolve of producer Saul Zaentz, who won his third Best Picture Oscar and the Thalberg award.

1996. *Romeo and Juliet* has had so many variations, it only proves the viability of the situation. Australian director Baz Luhrmann set the story in modern Miami. He kept some of the words and shot the film like MTV. Teenagers loved it. Why not, when the film had Leonardo DiCaprio and Claire Danes going for it?

1997. The remake of *Lolita* was held up, because distributors were wary of showing a child having sex—or because they figured there was no profit in the movie. Scripted by Stephen Schiff and directed by Adrian Lyne it had several virtues—including Melanie Griffith, Jeremy Irons, and Dominique Swain—but it all demonstrated that Nabokov's skill and eroticism was in his writing (and our reading).

1997. Paul Thomas Anderson was a spectacular new director. Only a few people saw his debut, *Hard Eight (Sydney)*, but his second film, *Boogie Nights*, was a hit. It was an affectionate survey of the world of pornography in the 1970s. The exceptional cast included Julianne Moore and Mark Wahlberg.

1994. And Woody Allen still managed a film in most years. *Bullets Over Broadway* (cowritten by Woody and Douglas McGrath) had a playwright (John Cusack) whose play has underworld support. Dianne Wiest won a supporting actress Oscar playing his star performer.

1994. *Forrest Gump,* from a novel by Winston Groom, was the story of a simple child who grows up to demonstrate that simplicity is better than wisdom. Robert Zemeckis directed and some detected a reactionary philosophy in Gumpism. Others settled for the rare charm of Tom Hanks in the lead. The Academy gave it Best Picture, Best Director, and an Oscar for Hanks.

1996. The Coen Brothers turned their eyes and ears to the north in *Fargo*. It was a violent picture about small crimes getting out of hand. But the tone was detached and nearly serene, thanks in great part to the Oscar-winning performance by Frances McDormand as the pregnant cop, Marge.

1996. *Sling Blade* was a haunting story about a retarded man who comes out of prison and makes friends with a kid. It was a triumph for Billy Bob Thornton who played the lead, wrote the script (and won an Oscar for it), and directed. He is seen here with Lucas Black.

1990s

1995. Terry Gilliam's *Twelve Monkeys* was an inspired piece of science fiction loosely based on French director Chris Marker's short film, *La Jetée* (1962). Brad Pitt plays an insane asylum patient and Bruce Willis a sociopath sent back in time to stop a deadly plague in the future.

1996. What is Drew Barrymore doing? She's screaming! *Scream*, directed by Wes Craven, was a new kind of horror flick for teens in which the language of the horror genre was spoofed—and then reprised in fresh gotchas. The franchise goes on.

1996. TV struck back, with the throbbing Lalo Schifrin theme music in *Mission: Impossible*. Brian De Palma directed, and the amazing box-office success was further proof of Tom Cruise's iconic status (he was producer, too). No, this isn't Tom writing the script.

1996. Writer-director Cameron Crowe made the sports agent into a modern (but happier) Willy Loman in *Jerry Maguire*. The fusion of comedy and truth worked because of the very sympathetic acting: by Renee Zellweger, Bonnie Hunt, Cuba Gooding Jr. (supporting actor Oscar), and Tom Cruise.

1990s

1995. **After years** of mainstream acting, Mel Gibson took it into his head to make a movie about the thirteenth-century Scottish hero, William Wallace. Then, by doing it the way Errol Flynn might have done, Mel made the world love the picture. But he directed it, too *(right)*, and *Braveheart* won Best Picture and Best Director.

1998. **Tom Sizemore** and Tom Hanks are about to lead their men ashore on D-Day, 1944 *(below)*. Steven Spielberg's *Saving Private Ryan* introduced new standards of realism in combat, but it was pledged to the rare sense of honor and duty in the Second World War.

1999. David O. Russell's *Three Kings* won many admirers. It was a story about the Gulf War that turned into a Capraesque fable—and it was all shot as if bleached out by heat and flame. The cast included George Clooney, Mark Wahlberg, Ice Cube, and Spike Jonze *(right)*.

1999. George Lucas had not directed a film personally since 1977 (with *Star Wars* itself). Some felt the rustiness showed in *Star Wars: Episode I – The Phantom Menace*. Not that the huge audiences complained. For the pioneer of special effects was still ahead of that game *(below)*.

1996. *Independence Day* was a version of the alien invasion story that climaxed in jazzy combat scenes and a "full" explanation of Area 51 on the Nevada Test Site. Roland Emmerich directed with a taste for laughs and action, and the cast included Will Smith, Bill Pullman, and Jeff Goldblum.

1996. Some franchises seemed unstoppable. The captaincy changed, but the Star Trek enterprise sailed on. This is *Star Trek: First Contact*, with Patrick Stewart as the new commander, Picard, and Alice Krige as the Borg Queen.

1997. In Robert Zemeckis's *Contact* (based on a Carl Sagan novel), Jodie Foster played a researcher who sends messages out into deep space, hoping for a reply. Well, she gets mail and takes a trip into some of the most sentimental special effects.

1997. Barry Sonnenfeld pulled off a very big hit with *Men in Black,* in which Will Smith and Tommy Lee Jones had to defend the Earth against countless grisly and comic alien invaders. It was a picture adored by children—and thus further proof that the old-fashioned kiddy movie was dead.

1999. "I see dead people." It was the secret to the surprise hit of the year, *The Sixth Sense*, that this line came not from a horror film but a meditation on death and spiritual kinship. The director, M. Night Shyamalan, drew remarkable performances from Bruce Willis and eleven-year-old Haley Joel Osment (who was up against Michael Caine for Best Supporting Actor).

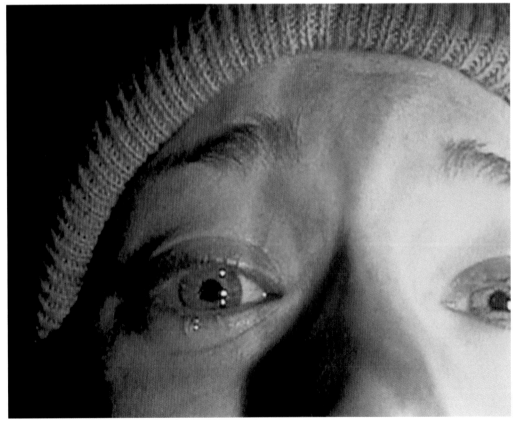

1999. *The Blair Witch Project* wasn't quite Hollywood, but its teenage following made the town take notice. It was a horror picture (purporting to be a documentary) in which the frightening things were never shown. Instead, the film turned on the fearful face—like that of Heather Donahue.

1998. Written by Andrew Niccol and directed by Peter Weir, *The Truman Show* was a fable about all the ways television has affected our society. The presence of Jim Carrey as Truman Burbank allowed for a lot of comedy, but some critics observed its unique sense of bright light and creeping anxiety. Ed Harris was the televsion producer who lovingly created the show in which life is live.

1999. Writer-director Frank Darabont stayed in prison. Why not, when the parable-like eloquence of *The Shawshank Redemption* was repeated in *The Green Mile*? Tom Hanks, Michael Clarke Duncan, and David Morse walk the mile.

1998. You can say *Shakespeare in Love* wasn't Hollywood—it was English. All true. But the American distributor, Miramax, turned it into the ideal Shakespeare for American tourists, thanks in part to Gwyneth Paltrow (the Miramax girl) as Will's love and inspiration. She got the Oscar for her work.

1999. Anthony Minghella made a riveting psychological thriller out of Patricia Highsmith's *The Talented Mr. Ripley*. Set in Europe in the 1950s, and based on stolen identity, the picture had dazzling acting from Matt Damon and Jude Law (seen here) as well as Cate Blanchett and Gwyneth Paltrow.

1999. Michael Caine won his second supporting actor Oscar as Wilbur Larch in *The Cider House Rules*. It was scripted by John Irving from his own novel, and directed by Lasse Hallström. Caine played the director of an orphanage, who wanted to leave his legacy to Tobey Maguire (one of the boys under his care).

1999. When Stanley Kubrick died, his work on *Eyes Wide Shut* was done. He had been years on this story of eroticism and marital fidelity—or otherwise. The result was beautiful, but even Kubrick enthusiasts were perplexed. Was it really that sexy? As for the stars, Tom Cruise and Nicole Kidman, their own marriage would not last much longer.

1999. The film of the year was *American Beauty*, a wistful study of suburbia. Alan Ball wrote the script and newcomer Sam Mendes (from England) was the director. The cast was headed by Annette Bening and Kevin Spacey (seen here with Mena Suvari). It won Best Picture, Director, Cinematography, and Screenplay, with an Oscar to Spacey, too.

1999. *Magnolia*, the next film by Paul Thomas Anderson, was an ambitious panorama of many lives in Los Angeles. The diverse cast included Jason Robards Jr., Tom Cruise, Philip Seymour Hoffman, William H. Macy, and Julianne Moore (seen here).

1999. Michael Mann's *The Insider* was about the man who blew the whistle on the tobacco industry and his relations with the TV show *60 Minutes*. Russell Crowe was the informer and Al Pacino played the show's producer.

1999. Alexander Payne's *Election* was a withering satire on high school and middle America. Matthew Broderick played the forlorn (and bee-stung) teacher who is destroyed by the implacable electability of Reese Witherspoon.

1999. Let the year and the century end with the astonishing invention of *Being John Malkovich* (directed by Spike Jonze). It was a film that showed how far the overarching fantasy of film had changed us. As well as JM and Cameron Diaz, it starred Catherine Keener and John Cusack.

2000s

2000. *Erin Brockovich* was based on a real case in which a single-mom paralegal took on Pacific Gas & Electric. But the movie was a perfect vehicle for Julia Roberts and enough to get her the Oscar that had always seemed likely. Steven Soderbergh directed and Julia was much helped by her costar, Albert Finney *(right)*.

2000. Writer-director Cameron Crowe delivered a charming portrait of his own days as a teenage writer for *Rolling Stone, Almost Famous (left).* The view of the rock scene may have been a little romanticized. Patrick Fugit played the boy, seen here with a group that includes Kate Hudson, Jason Lee, Fairuza Balk, Billy Crudup, and Anna Paquin.

2000. There hadn't been a good Roman movie for years. Ridley Scott's *Gladiator (previous pages)* mixed top-class costume research with computer-generated imagery so that Rome looked and felt as if it was being seen for the first time. It won Best Picture and brought an Oscar to Russell Crowe, who reaffirmed the widespread appeal of men in leather, armor, and short skirts.

2000s

The Future, the Meaning

In 1901, no one knew what Chaplin, Griffith or Garbo were going to mean to the world. But a hundred years later, the most far-reaching questions seem to depend on technology—how far will the success of *The Lord of the Rings* trilogy convert movies from a photo-based medium to a spectacle reliant on computer technology? Will our films get bigger and bigger? Or will they suddenly become smaller as we stay home and watch what we call "television"?

Films are more expensive than they have ever been—suppose they became absurdly cheap? Suppose one day, we put them on ourselves, like spectacles? Or suppose other media comes along—holographic happenings, interactive dreams, séances with the past and the future?

We still make old-fashioned films (*Titanic*); audiences seem drawn as much as ever to adventure (*Gladiator*); and we are eager to dream over possible futures (*The Matrix* films).

But something else was apparent by 2004: that the smaller "Independent" film had secured a place in America. There are viewers that want something more challenging, audiences that went to see *Traffic, Adaptation, Monster,* and even *The Passion of the Christ* (the defiant work of one man that for a long time had no distributor—and yet, in many ways, the kind of picture Cecil B. DeMille used to deliver).

The one thing close to certain is that the movies will prove to be the pioneer of some medium in which belief and business are so tangled that no one can separate them. In the end, that is Hollywood's legacy—the founding of a means of mass entertainment or nourishment in the tradition of air, food, sex, and sleep.

To be continued ...

2000. Senator John Glenn had gone back into space, so why not Clint Eastwood? In the leisurely, very enjoyable *Space Cowboys,* Clint directed himself, James Garner, and Tommy Lee Jones as veterans who come back to rescue the space program.

2000. How does a fishing boat survive a wave like that? But if the wave is so dangerous how can you film it? The answers are to be found in Wolfgang Petersen's *The Perfect Storm,* in which George Clooney captained the swordfish boat on its desperate voyage into the Atlantic (and the computer).

2000. Despite some feelings that *Cast Away* had ended up as an extended ad for Federal Express, millions went to see the Robert Zemeckis film, and came away impressed by Tom Hanks's ability to make a desert island seem like a place for conversation.

2000. *Traffic* was derived from a British television series, and it told several separate yet related stories about the global reach of the drug problem. Steven Soderbergh directed, and won the Oscar for his work. The all-star cast included Catherine Zeta Jones (all the better known for her marriage to Michael Douglas).

2001. Lecter was back again in Ridley Scott's *Hannibal*—but now the guy was amusing, a little seductive, and getting damn near adorable. What did it say about our feeling for villains that Lecter was now romantically drawn to Clarice Starling? Anthony Hopkins was riveting again, and Julianne Moore was his new fair lady.

2000. Actor Ed Harris got the notion that he was born to play abstract expressionist painter Jackson Pollock—in part because he looked a lot like Pollock. It was the first film he'd directed, and he had to put up a lot of his own money to get it done. But the response made it worthwhile and helped win an Oscar for Marcia Gay Harden playing Pollock's wife, Lee Krasner.

2001. *Blow* was another very strong treatment of the drug business, with yet one more dazzling performance from Johnny Depp in the lead. He is seen here with Penélope Cruz, further proof of the new interest in Hispanic performers.

2001. The Tom Cruise–Nicole Kidman marriage ended, but she had a great personal success singing, dancing, and acting as Satine, the courtesan, in Baz Luhrmann's highly original musical, *Moulin Rouge,* which mingled a theatrical turn-of-the-century Paris with much more modern songs.

625

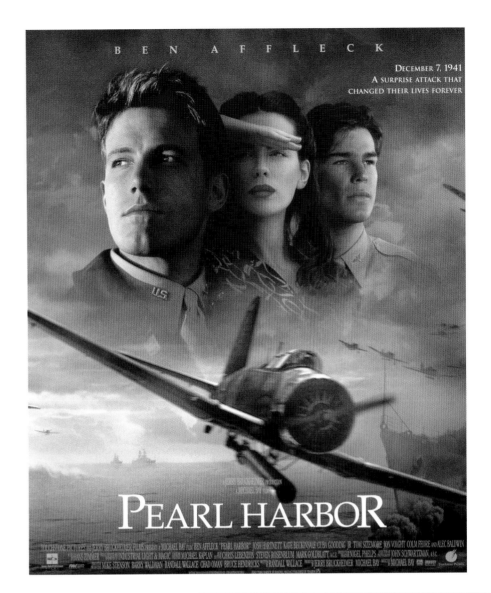

2001. And it was December 7, 1941 again as *Pearl Harbor* opened, directed by Michael Bay and produced by Jerry Bruckheimer. It had a love story that involved Ben Affleck, Kate Beckinsale, and Josh Hartnett, and it had explosions that seemed to last from here to eternity.

2001. The idea seemed familiar: an Earth where the Apes had taken over? *The Planet of the Apes* franchise came back, directed by Tim Burton, with Tim Roth (in helmet, *center*) as one of the stars putting on simian makeup.

2001. Since the earliest days, the movies have turned on our readiness to look at a face and feel for it. But suppose the face is not quite real? The picture was called *Final Fantasy,* but maybe it was the start of an entirely new kind of dream?

2001. The year would end, much as the movies had begun, with tales of mystery and imagination, wizards and magic. *The Lord of the Rings* was set for Christmas 2001, directed by Peter Jackson, and with Ian McKellen as the wizard Gandalf. How much will change in the next hundred years? How much will remain the same?

Photography Credits

225 (top) 20th Century Fox
(bottom) Warner Bros.
226 (top) 20th Century Fox
(bottom) MGM
227 MGM
228 (top) MGM
(bottom) Warner Bros.
229 MGM
230–31 MGM
231 Warner Bros.
232 (both) MGM
233 (both) MGM
234 Walt Disney
235 (both) Walt Disney
236 (both) Warner Bros.
237 Warner Bros.
238 (top) Kobal
(bottom) United Artists
239 (top) MGM
(bottom) Goldwyn/RKO
240 (top) United Artists.
(bottom) Republic
241 (top) 20th Century Fox
(bottom) Kobal
242 (top) RKO
(bottom) Warner Bros.
243 Warner Bros.
244 (top) Producers'
Releasing Corporation
(bottom) Universal
245 (top) MGM
(bottom) Universal
246 RKO
247 RKO
248–49 Columbia
249 Columbia
250 20th Century Fox
251 (top) RKO
(bottom) Robert
Coburn/Columbia
252 (top) 20th Century Fox
(bottom) RKO
253 MGM
254 Kobal
255 (top) Selznick/RKO
(bottom) United Artists
256 (top) Goldwyn/RKO
(bottom) MGM
257 (both) 20th Century Fox
258 (top) MGM
(bottom) Universal
259 (top) London Films
(bottom) Warner Bros.
260 Warner Bros.
261 (top) Warner Bros.
(bottom) George
Hurrell/RKO
262–63 RKO
263 MGM

1950s
264–65 Warner Bros.
266 MGM
267 MGM
268 (both) Paramount
269 Paramount
270 (top) Irving
Lippman/Columbia
(bottom) 20th Century
Fox

271 (top) 20th Century Fox
272 (bottom) MGM
273 (top) Paramount
(bottom) Warner Bros.
274 Universal
275 (top) Universal
(bottom) Allied Artists
276 (both) MGM
277 MGM
278 (top) Warner Bros.
(bottom) 20th Century
Fox
279 (top) Warner Bros.
(bottom) MGM
280 20th Century Fox
281 (top) Warner Bros.
(bottom) Magna
Theatres
282 (both) 20th Century Fox
283 (top) Paramount
(bottom) MGM
284 Warner Bros.
284–85 Warner Bros.
286 Columbia
287 (both) Columbia
288 (top) Paramount
(bottom) Columbia
289 Paramount
290 (top) Columbia
(bottom) United Artists
291 (both) United Artists
292 (top) Paramount
(bottom) Warner Bros.
293 Columbia
294 Warner Bros.
295 (both) Warner Bros.
296 (top) Warner Bros.
(bottom) Paramount
297 Paramount
298 (both) Paramount
299 Clarence Sinclair
Bull/MGM
300 (both) Paramount
301 (both) MGM
302 (both) Universal
303 20th Century Fox
304 (top) Stanley
Kramer/United Artists
(bottom) Paramount
305 (top) United
Artists/Hecht-Hill-Lancaster
(bottom) MGM
306 (top) Columbia
(bottom) Paramount
307 (both) Warner Bros.
308–09 Paramount
310 (top) 20th Century Fox
(bottom) Paramount
311 Paramount
312 (top) United Artists
(bottom) 20th Century
Fox
313 Columbia
314 MGM
314–15 MGM
316 (both) Paramount
317 (top) Columbia
(bottom) Paramount
318 MGM
319 Frank Powolny/20th
Century Fox

320 20th Century Fox
321 (top) 20th Century Fox
(bottom) Kobal
322 (top) Kobal
(bottom) Paramount
323 MGM
324 (top) United Artists
(bottom) Republic
325 (top) MGM
(bottom) Columbia
326 (both) United Artists
327 (top) United Artists
328 (top) MGM
(bottom) Disney
329 MGM
330 20th Century Fox
331 (top) 20th Century Fox
(bottom) Kobal
332 (top) United Artists
(bottom) Universal
333 (both) Columbia
334 (both) 20th Century
Fox
335 (both) United Artists

1960s
336–37 20th Century Fox
338 United Artists/Seven Arts
339 Landau-Unger
340 (both) Paramount
341 Paramount
342 Universal
343 (top) Alfred J. Hitchcock
Productions/Universal
(bottom) Universal
344 (both) United Artists
345 United Artists
346 (both) United Artists
347 United Artists
348 Mirisch-7 Arts/United
Artists
349 (both) Mirisch-7
Arts/United Artists
350 Columbia
351 (both) Columbia
352 (top) 20th Century Fox
(bottom) Allied Artists
353 Samuel Bronston
354 (top) Lion Prods.
(bottom) 20th Century
Fox
355 (both) Warner Bros.
356–57 Warner Bros.
358 (top) Warner Bros.
(bottom) United Artists
359 (top) United Artists
(bottom) Paramount
360 (both) Columbia
361 (top) Sam Shaw/Castle
Hill
(bottom) Embassy
362 (top) United Artists
(bottom) Columbia
363 (top) MGM
(bottom) Warner Bros.
364 (both) Bryna/Universal
365 (top) MGM
(bottom) Hawk Film
Productions/Columbia
366 MGM

367 (both) MGM
368 (top) Walt Disney
(bottom) 20th Century
Fox
369 Warner Bros.
370 MGM
371 (both) 20th Century Fox
372 (top) Warner Bros.
(bottom) Warner
Bros./Seven Arts
373 (both) Universal
374 Warner Bros.
375 (top) Columbia
(bottom) 20th Century
Fox
376 (top) Paramount
(bottom) Selmur/Cinema
Rel. Corp.
377 Paramount
378 Mirisch/United Artists
379 (top) Warner Bros.
(bottom) United Artists
380 (top) United Artists
(bottom) Columbia
381 Mirisch/United Artists
382 Warner Bros.
383 (both) United Artists
384 (top) Paramount
(bottom) Universal
385 (top) Embassy Pictures
(bottom) Paramount
386 (top) Warner Bros.
(bottom) 20th Century
Fox
387 (top) Columbia
(bottom) 20th Century
Fox/Chenault
388–89 Universal
390 (top) AIP
(bottom) MGM
391 (top) MGM
(bottom) Robert
Penn/Avco Embassy
392 Paramount
393 (both) 20th Century Fox
394–95 Image Ten
395 Latent Image Inc.
396 (top) Warner Bros.
(bottom) MGM
397 20th Century Fox
398 (both) Columbia
399 (top) Paramount
(bottom) Warner 7 Arts
400–401 Columbia
402 (top) Columbia
(bottom) United Artists
403 Palomar/ABC
404 20th Century Fox
405 (top) Columbia
(bottom) Cinerama

1970s
406–407 Columbia
408 20th Century Fox
409 United Artists/Fantasy
Films
410 (top) Paramount
(bottom) 20th Century
Fox
411 Cinema Center

Photography Credits

412 (top) Universal (bottom) 20th Century Fox
413 20th Century Fox/Warners
414 (top) 20th Century Fox (bottom) Simcha Prods.
415 (top) Paramount (bottom) 20th Century Fox
416 (top) Columbia (bottom) Warner Bros.
417 Paramount
418 (top) Warner Bros./Elmer Prods. (bottom) MGM
429 Warner Bros.
420 (top) Columbia (bottom) Avco Embassy
421 (both) Columbia
422 (both) Paramount
423 Paramount
424 (top) Warner Bros. (bottom) Universal
425 Warner Bros.
426 (top) Warner Bros. (bottom) 20th Century Fox
427 (top) United Artists (bottom) Columbia
428 (top) 20th Century Fox (bottom) MGM
429 (top) Solar/First Artists/National General (bottom) Sam Shaw/Faces International
430 (top) Columbia (bottom) Concord/Warner Bros.
431 (top) MGM (bottom) United Artists
432 Universal
433 (top) Universal (bottom) Paramount
434 (top) United Artists (bottom) ABC/Allied Artists
435 (top) Paramount (bottom) Robert Stigwood/Universal
436 (top) Paramount (bottom) Columbia
437 (top) Avco/Embassy (bottom) Zoetrope/UA
438 20th Century Fox/Aspen
439 (top) Warner Bros. (bottom) United Artists
440 Paramount
441 (both) 20th Century Fox
442 (both) Paramount
443 Steve Schapiro/Paramount
444 (top) Paramount (bottom) Steve Schapiro/Paramount
445 (both) Paramount
446 (top) Warner Bros. (bottom) 20th Century Fox
447 (top) 20th Century Fox (bottom) Falcon International

448 (both) Universal
449 (top) Universal (bottom) Columbia
450–51 20th Century Fox
451 20th Century Fox
452 (both) United Artists
453 (both) United Artists
454 Paramount
455 (top) Warner Bros. (bottom) United Artists
456 (top) Paramount (bottom) Warner Bros.
457 Columbia
458 (top) Columbia (bottom) United Artists
459 United Artists
460 (top) Warner Bros. (bottom) Columbia
461 (top) Columbia (bottom) United Artists
462 (top) United Artists (bottom) Warner Bros.
463 (top) Paramount (bottom) Columbia
464 (top) Lucasfilm/Coppola Co./Universal (bottom) Lucasfilm
465 (both) Lucasfilm/20th Century Fox
466 (top) MGM (bottom) Columbia
467 MGM
468 (both) Paramount
469 Paramount
470 EMI/Columbia/Warners
471 (top) Columbia (bottom) 20th Century Fox
472 Warner Bros.
473 (top) Orion/Warner Bros. (bottom) United Artists
474 (both) Paramount
475 (top) Columbia (bottom) 20th Century Fox/Columbia
476–77 United Artists
478 (both) Zoetrope/UA
479 Zoetrope/UA

1980s
480–81 Ron Phillips/Touchstone United Artists
482 Columbia
483 Columbia
484 (both) Paramount
485 (both) Warner Bros.
486 (top) Paramount (bottom) Michael Childers/20th Century Fox
487 (top) John Shannon/Paramount (bottom) Paramount
488 (both) Lucasfilm/20th Century Fox
489 Ralph Nelson, Jr./Lucasfilm/20th Century Fox
490 (top) Universal (bottom) Paramount
491 Warner Bros.

492 (top) Marcia Reed/Paramount (bottom) Brian Hamill/Orion
493 (top) Adger W. Cowan/Universal (bottom) Paramount
494 (top) Paramount (bottom) Orion
495 (top) Columbia/Mirage (bottom) Columbia
496 (top) Universal (bottom) ITC/Universal
497 (top) MGM (bottom) James Zenk/Universal
498 (top) 20th Century Fox (bottom) Zade Rosenthal/Paramount
499 (top) Kerry Hayes/20th Century Fox (bottom) Keith Hamshere/De Laurentiis
500 (bottom) Ladd Co./Warner Bros. (top) Stephen Vaughan/Ladd Co./Warner Bros.
501 (top) Universal (bottom) MGM/UA
502 (top) Walt Disney (bottom) New Line Cinema
503 Bob Penn/20th Century Fox
504 Paramount
505 (top) Paramount (bottom) Warner Bros.
506 (top) MGM/UA (bottom) Universal
507 (top) Universal (bottom) River Road Prods.
508 EMI/Antron Media
509 Zade Rosenthal/20th Century Fox
510 Paramount
511 (top) Warner Bros. (bottom) Universal
512 (top) Paramount (bottom) Christian Bale/Warner Bros.
513 Ladd Company/Warner Bros.
514 (top) TriStar (bottom) Orion
515 (top) Paramount (bottom) Gordon Parks/Warner Bros.
516 (top) Muky Munkacsi/Paramount (bottom) David James/MGM/UA
517 (top) Warner Bros. (bottom) David Appleby/Warner Bros.
518 Saul Zaentz Company
519 Warner Bros.
520 (top) Touchstone (bottom) Warner Bros.

521 (top) Universal (bottom) Forty Acres and a Mule Filmworks
522 (top) Joyce Rudolph/Orion (bottom) Keith Hamshere/Lucasfilm Ltd./Paramount
523 (top) Columbia (bottom) Amblin/Universal
524 (both) Brian Hamill/Orion
525 (both) Brian Hamill/Orion
526 (both) Columbia
527 (top) Ralph Nelson/Lucasfilm Ltd./Paramount (bottom) Lorey Sebastian/Gladden
528 (top) Frank Connor/Universal (bottom) Takashi Seida/Paramount
529 (top) Island/FilmDallas/Bountiful (bottom) De Laurentiis
530 (top) David Appleby/Enigma/Goldcrest (bottom) Ricky Francisco/Orion
531 (top) Warner Bros. (bottom) Roland Neveu/Universal
532 (top) Cannon (bottom) Zade Rosenthal/Paramount
533 (top) David Appleby/Orion (bottom) Steven Vaughan/United Artists
534 (top) Don Smetzer/Paramount (bottom) MGM/UA
535 Warner Bros.
536 (top) Andy Schwartz/Paramount (bottom) MGM
537 (top) Vestron (bottom) Warner Bros.
538 (top) TriStar (bottom) Universal/Gordon Joel Warren/Orion
539 Warner Bros.
540 Warner Bros.
541 (top) Rob McEwan/Paramount (bottom) Universal
542 (top) Andy Schwartz/20th Century Fox (bottom) Carolco
543 (top) Avenue (bottom) Murray Close/Lucasfilm Ltd./Paramount
544 Geffen/Warner Bros.
545 (top) Touchstone/Amblin (bottom) Warner Bros./DC Comics

546 (top) Brian Hamill/Orion (bottom) Outlaw
547 (top) Francois Duhamel/Touchstone (bottom) Zade Rosenthal/TriStar
548 (top) Columbia (bottom) Brian Hamill/20th Century Fox
549 (top) Jean Pagliuso/20th Century Fox (bottom) Andy Schwartz/Castle Rock/Nelson/Columbia
550 (top) Merrick Morton/TriStar (bottom) Anthony Barboza/Universal
551 Warner Bros.

1990s

552–53 Merie W. Wallace/20thCentury Fox/Paramount
554 Kimberly Wright/New Line Production
555 Jasin Boland/Warner Bros.
556 (top) Ron Batzdorff/Touchstone/Warners (bottom) Touchstone
557 Peter Sorel/Paramount
558 (top) 20th Century Fox (bottom) Barry Wetcher/Warner Bros.
559 (top) Cineplex Odeon (bottom) Peter Sorel/TriStar
560 (top) Merrick Morton/Castle Rock Entertainment (bottom) MGM/Pathé
561 (top) New Line (bottom) Phillip Caruso/Universal
562 (top) Ken Regan/Orion (bottom) Carolco
563 Orion/Paramount
564 Myles Aronowitz/Universal
565 (top) Columbia (bottom) Warner Bros.
566 (top) Orion (bottom) Warner Bros.
567 (top) Ben Glass/WB/Regency Enterprises V.O.F./Canal+ (bottom) Ben Glass/Universal
568 Firooz Zahedi/Carolco
569 (top) Zade Rosenthal/Warner Bros./DC Comics (bottom) David James/Paramount
570 Rico Torres/New Line/Dark Horse
571 (both) Disney
572 (top) Melinda Sue Gordon/Circle Films (bottom) Geffen Film Company

573 (top) Lorey Sebastian/Spelling Films International (bottom) BFI/Film on Four Int./Sankofa Film & Video
574 (top) David Lee/Warner Bros. (bottom) David James/Carolco/Canal+/RCS Video
575 (top) D. Stevens/Touchstone (bottom) Scott Del Amo/Esparza/ Katz Prod.
576 Columbia
577 (top) IRS Media, (bottom) Live Entertainment
578 (top) Columbia (bottom) Frank Connor/20th Century Fox/Morgan Creek
579 (top) Phillip Caruso/Columbia (bottom) Phil Bray/Buena Vista/Hollywood
580 (both) David James/Universal
581 Murray Close/Amblin/Universal
582 Ralph Nelson/Zoetrope/Columbia TriStar
583 (top) Francois Duhamel/Geffen Pictures (bottom) Sidney Baldwin/Warner Bros.
584 (top) Myles Aronowitz/MGM/Maiden /New Regency (bottom) Spelling/Fine Line
585 (top) Peter Iovino/Paramount (bottom) Kerry Hayes/Paramount/Capella/Cinehaus
586 (top) Louis Goldman/Columbia (bottom) Bruce McBroom/TriStar
587 (top) Louis Goldman/Columbia/TriStar (bottom) Zade Rosenthal/Lightstorm Entertainment
588 (top) Stephen Vaughan/Warner Bros. (bottom) Francois Duhamel/Paramount
589 (top) Bruce McBroom/Columbia/TriStar (bottom) Richard Foreman/20th Century Fox
590 Columbia/TriStar
591 (top) Ron Batzdorff/Universal (bottom) Richard Foreman/Hollywood Pictures

592 (top) Michael Weinstein/Castle Rock Entertainment (bottom) Peter Sorel/New Line Cinema
593 (top) Demmie Todd/Working Title/Havoc (bottom) Suzanne Hanover/United Artists
594 (top) Linda R. Chen/Miramax/Buena Vista (bottom) Phillip Caruso/Universal
595 (top) Linda R. Chen/Polygram/Spelling (bottom) Peter Sorel/Monarchy/Regency
596 (top) Elliott Marks/Paramount (bottom) Bruce McBroom/Universal
597 (top) Suzanne Tenner/TriStar (bottom) Glenn Watson/20th Century Fox
598 (top) George Kraychyk/Miramax (bottom) Barry Wetcher/Good Machine
599 (top) John Clifford/Fine Line Features (bottom) John Baer/TriStar/Gracie Films
600 (top) Phil Bray/Tiger Moth/Miramax (bottom) Merrick Morton/20th Century Fox
601 (top) Peter Sorel/Mario Kassar/Pathé (bottom) G. Lefkowitz/New Line Cinema
602 (top) Brian Hamill/Magnolia/Sweetland (bottom) Phillip Caruso/Paramount
603 (top) Michael Tackett/Working Title/Polygram (bottom) Michael Yarish/Miramax
604 (top) Phillip Caruso/Polygram (bottom) David M. Moir/Miramax
605 (top) Murray Close/Paramount (bottom) Andrew Cooper/Columbia TriStar
606 (top) Andrew Cooper/Icon/Ladd Co./Paramount (bottom) David James/Dreamworks LLC
607 (top) Murray Close/Warner Bros./Village Roadshow (bottom) Keith Hamshere/Lucasfilm
608 (top) 20th Century Fox (bottom) Elliott Marks/Paramount

609 (top) Francois Duhamel/Warner/Southside Amusement Co. (bottom) Columbia
610 (top) Ron Phillips/Hollywood Pictures (bottom) Artisan Pics.
611 (top) Melinda Sue Gordon/Paramount (bottom) Ralph Nelson, Jr./Castle Rock/WB
612 (top) Laurie Sparham/Miramax Films/Universal Pictures (bottom) Phil Bray/Paramount/Miramax
613 (top) Stephen Vaughan/Miramax (bottom) Warner Bros.
614–15 Lorey Sebastian/Dreamworks LLC
616 (top) Peter Sorel/New Line Cinema (bottom) Frank Connor/Touchstone Pictures
617 (top) Bob Akester/Paramount (bottom) Melissa Moseley/Universal

2000s

618–19 Jaap Buitendijk/Dreamworks/Universal
620 Neal Preson/Dreamworks LLC
621 Bob Marshak/Universal
622 (top) Warner Bros./Roadshow (bottom) Warner Bros.
623 (top) Zade Rosenthal/20th Century Fox/Dreamworks (bottom) Bedford Falls/Initial Ent.
624 (top) MGM/Universal/De Laurentiis (bottom) Demmie
625 (top) Lorey Sebastian/New Line/Avery Pix (bottom) 20th Century Fox
626 (top) Jerry Bruckheimer Films/Touchstone Pictures (bottom) David James/20th Century/Zanuck Co.
627 (top) Square Pictures (bottom) Pierre Vinet/New Line/Wingnut

Index

Index

Index

Index

Acknowledgments

The Kobal Collection

The Kobal Collection owes its existence to the vision, courage, talent, and energy of the men and women who created the movie industry, and those legacies live on through the films they made, the studios they built, and the publicity photographs they took. We collect, preserve, organize, and make available these photographs. Our success in this has helped sustain and enhance the reputations of the actors, filmmakers, photographers, designers, and studios as well as the films they created. We acknowledge their inestimable contribution and thank them for their continuing support.

The Kobal Collection would like to thank the editor, Barbara Berger, for her outstanding contribution to this fascinating project. Her skill in editing some of the most important and best-loved facets of our library is evident, what is perhaps less obvious is the indefatigable energy with which she helped us to unearth the rarer material in the archive, some of which has never been published before. Her unswerving dedication to finding exactly the right picture every time and maintaining the quality and integrity of this terrific book deserves our undying gratitude!

DK Publishing, Inc.

DK Publishing, Inc., would like to thank the following people at The Kobal Collection for their invaluable contributions, and for making this book possible: Lauretta Dives, Bob Cosenza, and Margie Steinmann. Special thanks go to Dave Kent, for his unflagging assistance in providing photographic material; archival staff members Phil Moad, Cheryl Thomas, Jamie Vuignier; and the website support of Sean Waterman, Chris Tomlinson, and Harriet Simpson at picture-desk.com.

We are grateful to David Thomson for his dedication and his brilliant, engaging text. Thanks also go to Timothy Shaner at Night & Day Design for his thoughtful design; Nanette Cardon at IRIS indexing; and photo credits compiler Joanna Roy.

Jacket images :
Front: *A Place in the Sun,* Paramount (c). Back: *2001: A Space Odyssey,* MGM (tc); *Easy Rider,* Columbia (cll); *Traffic,* Bob Marshak/Bedford Falls/Initial Entertainment (cl); *Gone With the Wind,* Selznick/MGM (cr); *Cabaret,* ABC/Allied Artists (crr).